They Don't Teach This In School

They Don't Teach This In School

MONEY LESSONS
For Toddlers to Teens!

DANNY KOFKE

Wyatt-MacKenzie Publishing
DEADWOOD, OREGON

They Don't Teach This in School
Money Lessons for Toddlers to Teens
Danny Kofke

ISBN: 978-1-939288-63-9

Wyatt-MacKenzie Publishing
DEADWOOD, OREGON

www.WyattMacKenzie.com

Dedication

This book is dedicated to the late Mike Kavanagh.
Your time here ended way too quickly but your love for
others continues to live on.

Table of Contents

Foreword

David Hatter, *President Invest-N-U*

Over the past 18 years, I have personally counseled thousands of adults on achieving their goals. I have learned a great deal about what lies in the hearts of real people, their real desires, their greatest fears, weaknesses and strengths. It is an incredible privilege to be allowed to peer into their hearts and help them establish a pathway for success. It is often an emotional connection. While many of the sessions begin with anger, embarrassment and defeat, nearly all of them end with forgiveness, confidence and optimism for the future. While there is an extraordinary sense of accomplishment that comes from setting a successful path for the future, there is also a sense of frustration (for them AND for me) with the time that has already been lost.

It pains me to see how much damage an adult can do to their finances before getting them on track. It also pains me to see how hard they have to work to undo decades of destructive, learned behavior regarding values and habits with money. If I could only go back and meet with them as a child…but I can't.

But YOU can.

This book provides a roadmap for you to teach and guide your children to develop healthy habits and values before they become an adult; before they begin making significant financial decisions that impact their future. Danny communicates in simple everyday terms. He will not confuse you with complicated financial terms or industry jargon and you will be richly rewarded for following his advice. Your children and the imprint they leave on the world will be one of your greatest legacies.

I have observed that a person on a mission is a force for powerful change. Unfortunately, the main obstacle for people pursuing their mission is often money. Parents can set their children up to BE on a mission, if only they can teach them healthy values and habits with money. Parents have an incredible opportunity to shape the future for their children and the thousands or millions of people their children will touch during their lifetime.

Teach your children how to get money out of their way and they WILL change the world.

Read this book and take Danny's advice. I can assure you that I will be giving it to every client of mine with children.

Introduction

Why There is a Need For This Book

"The best way to learn is to teach."
FRANK OPPENHEIMER

A recent study from the National Endowment for Financial Education surveyed 683 adults, aged 18 to 39, and 391 parents of adults in that age range. Forty-two percent of the adults said they are currently receiving or have received financial help from their parents, and 59% of parents said they've given.

I know that many people are hesitant to discuss money with their children (or their spouses/partners for that matter). I have talked about this with one of my pastors and he told me that people will come to him for help with all sorts of issues ranging from drug abuse to infidelity in a marriage but money issues still remain a taboo topic for a lot of people. I know that many parents are embarrassed by their past money mistakes and do not want to discuss these with their children. I feel the complete opposite—the mistakes are the reasons that we should ab-solutely discuss this topic with our children. Most kids love it when their parents mess up. They can relate to them a little better. As a parent, if you have made a money mistake, I feel it is a golden opportunity to help your child learn. You see, we all make mistakes. The important thing is that we learn from these mistakes and do not allow them to happen again.

I first really realized the need for this book in the fall of 2011. I had been on numerous TV and radio shows discussing how I teach my young children the basics of handling money, but the Occupy Wall Street Movement really opened my eyes and made me realize how little financial knowledge many older students have. I heard some in this movement were blaming "evil" corporations and CEOs for bad job prospects. Some recent college graduates had upwards of $50,000 in student loan debt (some much more) in fields where the prospect of finding a well-paying job is not likely for many. This is why many young people were angry—they had all this debt and a college degree but could only find a job as a barista at a coffee shop that paid next to nothing.

To further illustrate this point, there was an editorial written in a major city's newspaper from a local hometown young woman. She attended a four-year college-preparatory private girls' Catholic high school and then went on to earn degrees from two universities.

Upon graduating from college, she owed over $180,000 in student loan debt! She continued by acknowledging that the debt is her responsibility but she was able to accumulate this huge debt through a combination of factors including a lack of awareness. She now works two jobs and has a strict budget. Despite working more than most of us, she still lives with her parents because she cannot afford to have a place of her own. She feels as if she followed society's expectations, earned an education and is employed. Even though this is the case, she can barely afford to buy a meal out. She concludes that due to reckless neglect, student loan debt will be the financial ruin of her generation.

What a horrible situation to be in. After doing what she thought (and was probably told) was the correct course to follow, this young woman now realizes the errors of her decisions. It is too late for her to go back in time and follow a different path, but it is not too late for your child!

After reading about her and others who are in a similar situation, I started to think about how we (teachers) educate our students in money management. Looking back on my career I realized something awful—we DON'T! That's right, we will educate our youth on the characters in *Beowulf* or have them memorize the periodic table (things that many of us will never use outside of a high school classroom) but do not teach them how to balance a checkbook or create a budget. Now I could write another book on this topic but am pointing this out to you (the parent) so that you can hear it straight from the horse's mouth—your daughter/son will not learn about money management in school. If you want your child to have a healthy relationship with money, and if you do not want to end up like the 59% of parents who support their children into adulthood, it is up to you to teach the financial skills necessary to ensure this happens.

Most parents want their children to have the best education possible and try to teach them real-world skills. However, many of these same parents do not discuss (nor teach) personal financial matters with their children. The reason they don't discuss financial skills is not that they are bad parents. Most of us are so busy that we don't even think about talking about such matters with our children. In addition, many parents may not understand, or know how to teach, personal finance skills, or they themselves may have an unhealthy relationship with money. Even though we (adults) are not teaching our youth about money, they are still learning about this topic from a horrible teacher—advertisers.

According to the American Academy of Pediatrics, the

average American child sees almost 40,000 commercials every year! Since 1983, the annual amount of television advertising directed at kids has skyrocketed from just $100 million to more than $15 billion according to Juliet Schor, author of *Born to Buy: The Commercialized Child and the New Consumer Culture.* Companies spend large sums of money promoting their products and brands to kids for one reason—it works. Many kids can hum and sing commercial jingles by the time they turn three. By the time children reach age seven, they can recognize many companies' advertising logos and brand names.

Kids' preferences drive billions of dollars of spending by both their parents and them. With this constant bombardment of ads, plus a lack of financial education, is it any wonder that many children only know about spending, spending, spending, but know next to nothing about saving and investing?

Many of us develop our personal financial habits during our youth and these habits are similar to those of our parents. Adults who spend like there is no tomorrow and don't save for the future usually have children who are masterful at spending but horrible at saving.

According to a PNC financial independence survey released in March 2012, today's twenty-somethings have an average debt of $45,000 (this includes everything from cars to credit cards to student loans to mortgages). Even though many of our youth have struggled with financial literacy for years, schools have done next to nothing to fix this. According to a 2011 survey by the Council for Economic Education, fewer than half of the states make high school students take an economics class and just 13 require a personal finance class. In addition, just 16 states require testing in economics which is actually three fewer than in 2009. It seems we may be moving backwards when it comes to teaching financial matters to our youth.

Many adults do not know how to properly handle money. If you do not have the knowledge to manage your own finances properly, it will be very difficult to teach your children how to do so. As parents, most of us want our kids to have it better than we do. In order for that to happen, you have to take an active role in teaching your child how to manage money, because as I have just shared with you—they are not learning this anywhere else. Surveys show that parents, not teachers, have the greatest influence on a child's financial literacy. Even though this is a tough time for many, it is also a golden opportunity to make a lasting impact for the future of our country. We cannot change the past; but we can learn from our mistakes and make sure our children do not make the same errors. That is my goal in writing this book—to help you better prepare your child(ren) to thrive with their money.

Who I Am

I am currently a special education teacher in Georgia. I have taught for fourteen years and, in addition to teaching special needs students, have also taught pre-k, kindergarten, first grade and second grade. My love of teaching and finances led me to write two other personal finance books: *How To Survive (and perhaps thrive) On A Teacher's Salary* and *A Simple Book Of Financial Wisdom: Teach Yourself (and your kids) How To Live Wealthy With Little Money.*

My message has resonated well with others because I walk in the same shoes they do. My wife, Tracy, was a schoolteacher before becoming a stay-at-home mom for nine years to our two young daughters—Ava, currently 9, and Ella, currently 6 (Tracy got back into teaching in the fall of 2014). Despite living off a teacher's salary (a little above $40,000 here in Georgia) for nine years, we have no debt except our mortgage, we invest each month for our retirements, have a one-year emergency fund in place, and basically live "wealthy" lives on a moderate income.

As a result of my family's everyday approach to managing money, I have appeared on numerous television shows including *The CBS Early Show, Fox & Friends, The 700 Club,* CNN's *Newsroom,* HLN's *The Clark Howard Show,* Fox News Channel's *Happening Now,* CNN's *Your Bottom Line,* HLN's *Making It In America, MSNBC Live* and multiple shows on The Fox Business Network. I have also been interviewed on more than 400 radio shows and featured in many publications including *USA Today, The Wall Street Journal, The Atlanta Journal Constitution, Woman's Day,* AOL.com, CNN.com, Yahoo.com and MSNBC.com.

As a classroom teacher, I know firsthand that we (teachers) **do not** teach financial literacy to our students. It is because of this that I want to give you (the parent) the tools needed to become your child's financial teacher.

How This Book Was Written

I have divided this book into age groups. I have a section for the pre-school years (ages 3-5), the early elementary years (ages 6-8), the secondary elementary years (ages 9-11), the middle school years (ages 12-14), the high school years (ages 15-18) and the college/young adult years (ages 19 and up). I have also alternated between using the pronouns he and she when referring to your child to eliminate having to use he/she. Insert the appropriate gender as you read.

As a school teacher who has taught numerous grade levels, I know that you have to use different teaching styles for different age groups. Kindergarten students have much shorter attention spans than fifth graders so the lessons and activities have to be structured and taught as such. A high school student can learn the value of money firsthand by holding a job, whereas a 12-year-old needs to be taught in a way that relates best to her. Even though this book is divided into sections pertaining to specific age levels, you can discuss almost all these lessons with your child and teach to her specific needs.

When I taught first grade, the reading program I used was based on each student's individual needs. It is known as guided reading. There are leveled books (Levels A-Z) with Level A being the easiest and each level getting more advanced as they moved through the alphabet. The typical first-grade student was reading between Level D-J books. However, I had some students reading Level B books and others Level M books. The same holds true with this book. If your child is 10 years old but cannot grasp the concepts discussed in chapter six, go back a chapter or two and teach the skills discussed in that chapter and then move forward. By no means is the order of the chapters and lessons set in stone— teach the skills that are most appropriate for your child.

Who Should Read This Book

This book is geared towards every parent who wants their child to grow up and live differently than many of us have. We have all made money mistakes that have created setbacks in our lives and put us somewhat behind the eight ball. The cause of many of these mistakes was something other than not being "smart enough." In fact, there are many "smart" people who have made horrible mistakes when it comes to managing money. Many of these mistakes were made because of a lack of knowledge.

As mentioned before, schools do a horrible job of teaching financial literacy. Add to this the fact that money topics remain taboo for many families and you can easily see why so many people struggle when it comes to handling money correctly.

What if you could give your child some tools to help her avoid some of the money mistakes you've made? That is the purpose behind this book—to help you give your child a head start on the path to financial success.

What This Book Can Accomplish

How many of us have said, *If I only knew then what I know now?* Pretty much every one of us. This book can eliminate that phrase from your child's vocabulary when it comes to handling money.

Taking a look at current headlines, most of us can see how poor many countries' financial situation is. I do not know what the future holds, but if we go by current economic predictions, it is going to be much more difficult for our children to become financially successful than it was for previous generations. We need to change the way we view and handle money. This book is the starting point to forming the habits and values of a financially knowledgeable individual. Your child is watching and eager to learn—let's go!

"Teach your children how to get money out of their way and they WILL change the world."

DAVID HATTER

Section 1

Laying The Foundation

In the following chapter, I lay the foundation for your child's financial success. I will go over some of the healthy values and habits that people who have success with money possess. I hope these habits and values will give you some guidance when teaching your child about money.

CHAPTER 1

20 Healthy Values And Habits That Lead To Financial Success

It pretty much goes without saying that if someone wants to have success with money, he or she needs to have sound habits and values related to money. Let me quote from the most circulated book of all time, *The Holy Bible*:

> "Therefore everyone who hears these words of mine and puts them into practice is like a wise man who built his house on the rock. The rain came down, the streams rose, and the winds blew and beat against that house; yet it did not fall because it had its foundation on the rock. But everyone who hears these words of mine and does not put them into practice is like a foolish man who built his house on sand. The rain came down, the streams rose, and the winds blew and beat against that house and it fell with a great crash." *Matthew 7: 24-27*

Powerful words that still hold true more than 2,000 years later! Could we relate these words to our current housing crisis? Maybe if more people took this advice and bought homes they could truly afford (building a house on rock rather than easy credit) the foreclosure rate, which has led to this crisis, would be lower.

Before going any further, let's look at the definition of a value and habit:

VALUE
A principle, standard or quality considered worthwhile or desirable.

HABIT
A recurrent often unconscious pattern of behavior acquired through frequent repetition.

Now that we know what each of these means, let's take a look at some of the values and habits that lead to success with money. I have listed 20 healthy values followed by the healthy habits which correlate to these habits. Notice how the principles we possess lead us to develop certain habits that frame how we handle money.

#1

HEALTHY VALUE
Don't Worry About What Others Have

HEALTHY HABIT
Establishing Priorities

"Keeping Up With the Joneses" is one of the reasons so many are in financial trouble right now. People try to emulate those who they think have it all, and therefore buy things they cannot afford in order to look good on the outside. This is like watching a duck swimming on the water. On the surface, it looks very peaceful and effortless; however, below the water, the duck is moving its webbed feet as fast as possible and it does not look so peaceful. Your neighbor may seem to "have it all" yet can't sleep at night because of how much debt he is in. Doing what is right for you (and not someone else) is a value many "wealthy" people possess.

Having this value will lead you to setting priorities for you and your family. Most of us can't have it all so we have to choose what is most important and go down the list. Recently, Tracy came home and told me that some friends of ours had bought a brand new car. Then she said that *we would probably never get a chance to drive a vehicle with that new car smell.* I said, "That's not true; we do hope to one day have a new car. But right now our priority is to invest for our futures instead. We could spend what we invest each month on a car payment but, thirty years from now, that car will be long gone and we would have nothing to show for it. Instead, we invest our money so that one day we will be able to buy a new car (probably a lot fancier one than we would today) outright and still have money in the bank." It is easy to get caught up in things that we don't have—making a list of what is important to you helps you stay the course.

#2

HEALTHY VALUE
Sacrifice/Delayed Satisfaction

HEALTHY HABIT
Have and Work A Plan

The value of "Sacrifice/Delayed Satisfaction" ties in with the value listed previously. I sacrifice today for tomorrow. I make the conscious decision to invest money that I could easily use to purchase some of those things I would like to have today. This is easier said than done but, wanting to eventually become self-sufficient requires one to give up some immediate gratification for delayed satisfaction.

Since this is one of my values, I have and work my plan accordingly. I would like to retire someday and still be able to enjoy life so I need to have a plan in place and work this plan to make my vision become reality. If I focused on buying everything I wanted right now, and did not set money aside to be invested for my future, my Golden Years would not be everything I want them to be. Delaying satisfaction and sticking to my plan will (hopefully) enable me to continue living the way I want to once I stop working.

#3

HEALTHY VALUE
Earning

HEALTHY HABIT
Earning

"Earning" is both a value and habit. While it may seem easy for those who earn a lot of money to do well financially, each of us has a unique earning power. Those who make a large salary have (usually) utilized the gifts they were given and used these qualities to earn as much as they can.

When earning money becomes a habit, you are looking at ways to boost your income. It may require more time and sacrifice but the money earned can be well worth your efforts. For example, as a teacher I have some earning power outside the classroom. I have had the opportunities (and taken advantage of these) to raise my earnings by teaching in the after-school program, tutoring students and even teaching summer school.

#4

HEALTHY VALUE

Self-Sufficiency/Independence

HEALTHY HABIT

Focus On Net Worth/Work On Independence

Being responsible for yourself and not relying on someone else to take care of your needs—this value may be hard to recognize early on, but we should all strive for it. While I am somewhat confident that my pension (as a teacher I am one of the few who still has this luxury) and Social Security will be there in some form when I retire, I am not dependent on these. I invest each month for my retirement, so I will not have to solely rely on either of these to take care of *all* of my expenses later on in life.

When one focuses on his net worth rather than trying to accumulate more stuff, he is working on this value. Net worth is the amount of money you are actually worth after subtracting what you owe compared to what you own. To illustrate this more, take a look at the following list:

Debts (What You Owe)

House/Mortgage	$100,000
Car	$20,000
Student Loan	$15,000
Credit Cards	$10,000

Credits (What You Own)

Retirement Account	$25,000
Savings Account	$5,000
Checking Account	$2,000
Savings Bonds	$1,000

When figuring out net worth, in many cases you can subtract your debts from your credits. However, when there are houses and cars involved, you can estimate (be realistic here) how much you could sell each of these for. For the example on the previous page, we will say you could reasonably sell your home for what you owe on it so that will make that a zero balance. We will say you could get $10,000 for your car so after selling it you would still owe $10,000 on this loan, which is the amount we will use in determining the net worth. When we add up the remaining debts we get a total of $35,000. Next, we add up the credits to get $33,000. In this case, the debts are greater than the credits so we subtract what we own from what we owe and have a net worth of negative $2,000—YIKES!

I point this out because people who have this value understand it is not what you have that counts, but rather what you actually own that determines how independent you will become.

#5

HEALTHY VALUE
Doers vs. Dreamers

HEALTHY HABIT
Set Goals

Most of us know of folks who always have the best plans in place but are hesitant to act on them. They can come up with reasons that they need something to happen first before they can carry out their great plans. I once read a great quote on this: "It is direction, not intention, that determines destination." Being a "doer" instead of a "dreamer" is a powerful value to possess.

Setting and writing down goals is a wonderful habit to develop. This is not only true with money management but also in many areas of your life. There are countless stories of people who wrote down their goals, viewed and focused on them routinely, and ultimately saw the goals become accomplishments.

Writing down your goals gives you a sense of urgency—it is much harder to disregard something in your view at all times. It is great to dream, but those who become successful take action to make these dreams a reality. Like the old Nike slogan says, "Just Do It!"

#6

HEALTHY VALUE
Recognize Roadblocks/Avoid Self-Sabotage

HEALTHY HABIT
Set Yourself Up For Success

We all have areas in which we lack some control—recognizing these roadblocks and avoiding self-sabotage is another strong value. For example, I have a weakness for Krispy Kreme doughnuts. Knowing this, I choose not to stop by one of their stores when I see their sign lit up displaying a fresh batch that just came out of the deep fryer. Knowing and staying away from your weaknesses might be the most important habit to develop.

We could obviously apply this to other areas besides money (food, drugs, etc.) but those who are successful with money put themselves in situations which help them succeed. It may be tempting, and even thrilling, to invest a large sum of money on the newest and most talked-about stock (recently Facebook is an example of this), but most wealthy people realize while this may work, many times it will not. Because of this, they use the method that has led many to financial success—investing a set amount each month in mutual funds over a long period of time. While this practice may not generate interesting talk at a cocktail party, it is the path that most financially successful people have used to build their wealth.

#7

HEALTHY VALUE
Spend Less Than You Make

HEALTHY HABIT
Budgeting/Pay Cash

Spending less than you make seems so easy on paper, but it is a very difficult value to develop. No matter how much money you earn, if you spend more than you have coming in, you will eventually be broke (if only our Congressmen understood this). Warren Buffet is a great example of someone who has this value. Even though he is worth more than anyone I know, he still lives in the modest home he bought over 30 years ago. It is easy to constantly *up* your spending with every raise you receive, but living *up to your means* is a recipe for disaster. No one plans for a salary reduction or job loss but it happens (quite frequently in the past few years). Unfortunately, many people did not see the importance of this value until it was way too late. Going back a generation or two, our parents/grandparents never bought things on credit since there was no credit available. That was a GOOD thing as it forced folks to save up to afford things and not go in debt for them.

Having a budget is a habit that people who spend less than they earn possess. Knowing how much money you have to spend and staying in this range leads to financial success;

spending money without any limits leads to financial disaster. To develop a budget, you need to know what you are spending money on. A great way to do this is to walk around with a sheet of paper and pencil for one month and write down everything you buy. At the end of the month, you can analyze this list and see exactly where your money is going. You may even see an area or two you can cut out which will put more money back into your pocket.

Using cash is a great way to stay within budget. Many of us have more of an emotional attachment to cash compared to a piece of plastic. Try it for yourself the next time you go to buy something—pay cash and see if you feel differently. A good way to start using cash is, after tracking your spending and seeing how you are spending your money and how much you need in a given week, take this exact amount every week. This amount will be all you can spend for the week. This is also a lot easier said than done, but is a great habit to follow.

#8

HEALTHY VALUE
Self-Control

HEALTHY HABIT
Sleep On It

Self-control helps you walk away from those items which are sure to lead to destruction. Many of us, because we lack self-control, knowingly buy things we truly cannot afford.

"Sleeping on it" is a habit people with self-control have. When we get caught up in the moment, it is pretty easy to make an irrational decision and cause ourselves financial harm. The key is being able to walk away and think about it. Instead of buying something you desire the first time you see it, I challenge you instead to walk away and think about this for 24 hours. I bet you will spend a lot less money applying this habit.

#9

HEALTHY VALUE
Purpose

HEALTHY HABIT
Greater Good

Having a sense of purpose helps us continue on our path despite the many setbacks along the way. When your purpose is bigger than just serving yourself, you will find it easier to achieve your goals because you are working for reasons greater than self-serving ones.

Working for the greater good is a natural habit of this value. An example of this is one of my good friends, David. Years ago David was living what many would call the American Dream. He made a nice salary, lived in a house with a lot of square footage, drove a Mercedes and even had an airplane. However, he was not serving the greater good and, thus, felt he was not following his purpose. He decided to start his own business to help schoolteachers keep more of their hard-earned investment dollars. This required a huge sacrifice. He sold most of his stuff and his family had to move in with his in-laws. The first few years of this venture were pretty tricky to say the least. There were many nights when David wondered if his plan would work. However, since he had a great sense of purpose, he stuck with his goal and has made a tremendous change in the way hundreds of thousands of teachers invest their money and he will continue to change more lives because of his purpose.

#10
HEALTHY VALUE
Driven To Succeed

HEALTHY HABIT
Sticking To A Commitment

It pretty much goes without saying that most successful people are driven. They have a strong work ethic which can lead to financial success.

A common habit of these individuals is that they stick to the commitments they make—both to themselves and others. If you want to handle money better, hold yourself accountable and do not settle for less. Make a commitment to yourself that you will not accept any more excuses for your financial mistakes. Learn from these mistakes and uphold your promise.

#11
HEALTHY VALUE
Patience

HEALTHY HABIT
Waiting

I have to admit, this is something I am not very good at and am still working on. Having patience can seem to run directly against one of the other values we discuss—being driven. However, sometimes we just have to sit tight and let things play out the way they are supposed to. When you have done all you can do, the only thing left is to be patient and see how it works out

When you are patient, you are able to wait. This is how many people retire with a sizable nest egg; they invest a set amount of money every month for a number of years, and after thirty years, have a good amount of money. They do not try to time the market and speculate on the next big thing; rather, they are patient and let compound interest work its magic.

#12

HEALTHY VALUE
Honesty With Self and Others

HEALTHY HABIT
Talk About It/Being Open

Honesty is very important in all areas of life—especially when it comes to money. My 9th grade Civics teacher used to preach that "honesty is the best policy" and now, more than ever, I fully understand why this is so.

Many people were not honest with themselves when it came to purchasing certain items. Deep down they knew they could not truly afford something, but by being dishonest with themselves, justified they could. The results have been disastrous! Today we have thousands of foreclosed houses and people who are worse off now than they were in the past. If they had been honest with themselves, they would not be facing such dire situations right now.

It is also important to be honest with others. I look at someone like Bernie Madoff to illustrate this. He was dishonest and ruined thousands of lives through his ponzi scheme. I am sure times were good for Bernie for quite a while, but eventually he got caught and will spend the rest of his life behind bars. He was not open with his investors and is now paying a price (although I think he may have gotten off pretty easily compared to some of the people he ripped off). Even if he had never been caught, I cannot imagine going to bed every night knowing that I was ruining others' lives.

We will all die one day. Wealthy people know that money will come and go but being honest will follow them many years after they are gone.

#13

HEALTHY VALUE
Creating A Legacy

HEALTHY HABIT
Sharing/Giving

This value correlates with being honest—dishonesty is not a legacy that many hope to leave behind. Creating a legacy does not necessarily mean leaving a lot of money to your children or establishing a scholarship in your name (although these are two things that I would love to be able to do in the future). Creating a legacy is leaving this world a better place. It can be something like writing a book or donating your time to a soup kitchen.

I will admit right off the bat that I am not a big fan of others telling me what I should do with my money and/or time. I, like some of you, get pretty angry when I am told what I "should" be doing with my hard-earned money or precious time. However, when you are able to give some money and/or time to a cause you are passionate about, the pay-off is much greater than any dollar amount you could place on it. There are numerous examples of celebrities who give huge amounts of money to various causes. You can easily do a search for these to find out their reasons; however, I want to share a personal story about giving.

After graduating from high school, I attended a local

community college and lived at home during this time. Since this was the case, there were not many expenses I had to pay for (a great way to build financial success but more on that in future chapters). After my first semester, I sold my textbooks back to the college bookstore. I had earned a scholarship that had paid for these books so this money was, in essence, free money. Around this time (it was near Christmas), my local newspaper ran a few stories about people who were struggling and could use some extra money to help them.

Now, I could have gone out and blown this money on things that were not so good for me, but I read one person's story that caught my attention. There was a mentally handi-capped gentleman who lived in a group home who was in need of a bike to get around town. I decided to use the money I got from selling my college textbooks to help him buy a bike. I sent it off to the newspaper and it felt good. On Christmas morning, on the front page of the paper, was a picture of this man riding his new bike with the biggest smile I have ever seen. To this day, whenever I think about this, it brings tears to my eyes. I don't remember how much money I was able to give but it left me with a lasting impression on how big of a payback we can receive when we are able to give.

#14
HEALTHY VALUE
Courage

HEALTHY HABIT
Confidence

Many things that we do in life require courage. Change is always hard, but if something was easy to do then everyone would be doing it. I think of the courage my family had when we moved from Florida to Georgia in 2006. We moved away from family, friends, a job and the county I was born in. We wanted to move somewhere where we could experience four seasons but also knew that it would benefit us financially. The cost of living had gone up in Florida and, it was at this point in time, when the housing market was strong. We had a goal for Tracy to be able to be a stay-at-home mom for as long as possible and this move would help us achieve that. While this move was scary for us, we did have the courage to do it and have benefitted from this move in many ways.

Having confidence enables us to make changes that require courage. While we cannot always be sure if we are making the right decision, being confident helps us see the best in most decisions we make.

#15

HEALTHY VALUE
Simplicity – Needs vs. Wants

HEALTHY HABIT
Rainy Day Savings – Things You Can't Plan For

Knowing the true difference between "Needs" and "Wants" is a value that leads to financial success. Many people think they need something and spend money they do not have to obtain it when, it turns out, this need was only a want. For instance, I know people who feel a cell phone is a need when, less than ten years ago, they did not have one. Now, not only do they have to have one but this phone has to be the newest one with the most apps.

Many of us know how important it is to save, but sometimes the reasons for saving are not even known to us. I am in the position to be writing this book because Tracy and I had rainy day savings. I had never given a thought to writing my own book. A number of years ago, some of my colleagues said that Tracy and I did well with money and suggested I write a book detailing this. I decided to write my first book— *How To Survive (and perhaps thrive) On A Teacher's Salary*— by paying an upfront fee with a publishing company. Since I was an unknown author I completely understood why I had to invest in myself to become published. Because Tracy and I had a rainy day fund, I was able to make this investment. This investment got me started on doing what I am passionate about—helping others with money. In fact, that first book has opened many doors for me!

Having money to invest in myself has enabled me to publish more books at no cost to me (with more on the way); meet numerous people and become friends with some who have a great influence on me; appear on national television more than 25 times; be interviewed on more than 400 radio shows; help others change their financial habits; and experience other opportunities that have not come my way yet. I now look back at the past seven years since *How To Survive* came out and all of the cool things that have happened because I had money set aside for an unplanned opportunity. I have had a few breaks and been fortunate, but I am a firm believer that luck happens when opportunity meets preparation. Having a rainy day fund can help more opportunities happen in life.

#16

HEALTHY VALUE
Avoid Destructive Debt – Knowing The Difference Between Good and Bad Debt

Invest In Things That Increase In Value

This may seem like a "no brainer" but those who are successful with money usually know the difference between bad debt and good debt.

While I do feel it should be a goal to be completely debt-free, there are instances when it is a good idea to take on debt. For instance, when purchasing a house. Most of us do not have $100,000 or more just sitting around so we take out a loan (a mortgage) to buy a house. Over time, for most Americans, this turns out to be a very good investment. Other debts that can be considered good debt include student loans, a loan to start a business, and a loan to invest in real estate. While such types of loans are not guaranteed to make you money, you have a chance that the original amount borrowed will appreciate, or will increase your earning power, and help you make a lot more money than the amount of the loan.

A habit that many wealthy people follow is investing in items that go up in value and do not automatically depreciate. I recently spoke with someone who bought a brand new car. He said he could not resist buying new because he got a great deal. While I did not say anything to him (sometimes it is best to keep quiet depending on who you are talking to) when I got home I thought about it. This "great deal" costs around $20,000 today, but ten years from now, this same car will be worth less than $10,000! Doesn't sound like such a great deal now, huh? Many broke people continue to make decisions that keep them broke whereas wealthy people continue to act in ways that made them wealthy to start with. Investing in things that appreciate, and not depreciate, in value is a great way to become rich.

#17

HEALTHY VALUE
Frugality

HEALTHY HABIT
Stretch It/Track Your Spending

I have to admit that I kind of chuckle at this value— being frugal was considered an insult as little as ten years ago. I know this firsthand because I have been frugal most of my adult life (probably even in my teen years, too). I have been told things such as "You only live once" or "Get off your wallet." Since I had my eyes on my family's future and what was right for us, I was able to let these comments slide pretty easily.

Interestingly, about five years ago being frugal started to become cool. Many people were looking to live on less, and all of a sudden, it was considered a compliment to be frugal. I know many people now even look at others who spend money they don't have as being foolish instead of wanting to emulate, and try to keep up with, them.

Being able to stretch your income is a great habit to have. No matter how much money we make, most of us would like a little more. Being able to stretch your salary as far as possible enables you to have more money left at the end of the month.

Tracking your spending can help you stretch your money as far as possible. I have talked to people in the past and they will tell me they would like to start investing or saving money but just do not make enough. When I take a closer look, they say they do not make much money but have the newest phone or latest designer clothes. Many of us make enough money but choose to spend it in ways that hurt our bottom line.

If you write down everything you spend for a month, at

the end of the month you can see exactly where your money went. Many become surprised to learn they spent $100/month on specialized coffee or lunches out. Once you have the knowledge of where your money is going, you can cut back where needed.

#18

HEALTHY VALUE
Gratefulness

HEALTHY HABIT
Appreciate What You Have – Stop and Smell The Roses

I know this is another value that is easier said than done, but we all have things that we can truly be grateful for; the key is to recognize these things. With the constant media bombardment, it is so easy to get caught up in all that we want and don't have. At these times, we need to take a large-picture look to realize how blessed we are.

One of the most memorable experiences I had in my life was living in Poland. Shortly after getting married, Tracy and I accepted jobs to teach in the city of Krakow. We were able to live a different life than most for the first two years of our marriage. We saw firsthand how many Polish families were much happier than many of our American friends even though our friends back home had much more stuff. This really made an impact on us and set the stage for how we would live our lives. We realized that while stuff is nice to have, it is not the end-all be-all. We walked to and from school most days and spent a lot of time reflecting and talking. Even though we now have two children, and life is a lot more hectic now than it was then, we can still tap back into that period of our lives when we need to regroup. A wonderful saying that I refer to often is, "Want what you have and you will always have what you want." 'Nuff said!

#19

HEALTHY VALUE
Routines – Pay Yourself First

HEALTHY HABIT
Multiple Accounts

Many of us work extremely hard yet have little to show for our efforts. In fact, we pay everyone else (the car company, bank for our mortgage loan, etc.) before we pay ourselves, and we usually end up with nothing set aside for us to enjoy. This is why it is so important to pay yourself first—to ensure you have something to show for the fruits of your labor.

Having multiple accounts is a great way to make sure you have money set aside for the many types of purchases that come along. You can have accounts for items such as a vacation fund, Christmas fund and car insurance. By paying yourself first and placing the proper amount of money in each of these accounts, you can set yourself up for success when it comes time to pay these bills.

#20

HEALTHY VALUE
Prioritizing

HEALTHY HABIT
Use Money As A Tool To Build Wealth

Raising a family on a teacher's salary (around $42,000 a year) can be difficult at times and prioritizing is key. It is hard to complain because, in these tough economic times, many people would love to have that amount coming in. However, I bet most of you agree that supporting a family of four on that amount does take some discipline. Despite making this nominal amount for a number of years, Tracy and I have no debt except our mortgage; we invest each month for our retirement; we have an emergency fund in place; and basically we live "wealthy" lives on a moderate income. You see, it isn't always how much you make, but rather what you do with what you make.

I have talked to numerous people who tell me they wish they had enough money to save for retirement or put away for an emergency. They go on to explain that they do not have any extra money. However, they drive a brand new car or have the newest iWhatever. I go on to explain that they do have this "extra" money but are choosing to spend it, rather than investing in themselves.

Sure it is difficult to set money aside instead of purchasing that newest gadget the media and our friends tell us we have to have, but most of us *do* make enough money to build wealth. Instead of building wealth, we choose to spend it on things that do the complete opposite. People who choose to use their hard-earned money to build up their emergency funds and/or retirement accounts instead of purchasing items for the here-and-now are those who end up becoming wealthy after a number of years.

Summary

I know this is probably a lot to take in, and you may feel it will be difficult to teach these habits/principles to your children, because if you are like many, you don't even possess all of these yourself. That is okay! The goal here is to illustrate as many habits and principles as possible so that you can try to start instilling them in your child.

This list is not meant to be the end-all-be-all and I am sure I overlooked other important habits and principles. I want you to keep these in mind with the lessons discussed later on in the book. Please do not feel overwhelmed—by taking the time to read this book you are already ahead of many others in building a bright financial future for your child(ren)!

Section 2

How Do Children Learn and What Do They Know

The next two chapters will show you the characteristics of the three learning styles (visual, kinesthetic and auditory) and will give you a quiz to determine your child's unique style, so you can best reach her when using the tools provided in following chapters.

There is also a quiz for you to give your child. This is geared towards older children (12 and up), but feel free to use it with your child no matter his age so you can see first-hand the knowledge they have when it comes to certain financial issues.

CHAPTER 2
Visual, Kinesthetic or Auditory?

What Type of Learning Style Best Suits My Child?

Since I am a teacher, I wanted to briefly discuss the three main types of learning styles and why it is important for you to know which style best suits your child(ren).

The three basic learning styles are visual, auditory and kinesthetic. Here are the basic characteristics of each:

Visual learners prefer using images, pictures, colors, and maps to organize information and communicate with others. They can easily visualize objects, plans and outcomes in their mind's eye. They also have a good spatial sense, which gives them a good sense of direction. They can easily find their way around using maps, and rarely get lost. When they walk out of an elevator, they instinctively know which way to turn. A visual learner loves drawing, scribbling and doodling, especially with colors. They typically have a good dress sense and color balance (although not always).

Auditory learners like to work with sound and music. They have a good sense of pitch and rhythm and can typically sing, play a musical instrument or identify the sounds of different instruments. Certain music invokes strong emotions in an auditory learner. They notice the music playing in the background of movies, TV shows and other media. They often find themselves humming or tapping a song, or a theme or jingle pops into their head without prompting.

Kinesthetic learners prefer to use their bodies and sense of touch to learn about the world around them. They typically like sports and exercise along with other physical activities such as gardening or woodworking. They like to think out issues, ideas and problems while exercising and/or moving. They are more sensitive to the physical world around them and notice and appreciate textures, for example in clothes or furniture. When learning a new skill or topic, a kinesthetic learner would prefer to jump in and play with the physical parts as soon as possible. They would prefer to pull an engine apart and put it back together, rather than reading or looking at diagrams about how it works. The thought of sitting in a lecture listening to someone else talk is not pleasant for this type of learner. In those circumstances, they fidget or can't sit still for long—they want to get up and move around.

What Type Of Learner Is My Child?

Many of you probably have a good idea in which of the above mentioned categories your child fits best. To help you a little more, answer the following questions and then score your child based on each answer:

1. You and your child take a trip to the pet store. The manager takes an adorable puppy out of the cage so that you and your child can "get to know him." Which of the following ways would your child be most likely to interact with the dog?

    A. He'd watch the dog's every move intently.

B. He'd immediately start petting the dog and engaging in a sort of play.

C. He'd talk to the dog and try to communicate with it.

2. You want to spend quality time with your child. So you ask her what type of game she'd like to play with you. She's most likely to recommend:

A. An active game.

B. A fun word game.

C. A video game.

3. You're having an important conversation with your child about the importance of not getting into the car with strangers. While you're talking, your child is most likely to:

A. Listen to you without budging.

B. Not be able to give you her full attention.

C. Watch your lips moving and your gesticulations.

4. Every child likes to have Mom or Dad read them a good book. But your child especially enjoys reading books with you when:

A. You read the book to him out loud and take on interesting character voices.

B. He pretends to be certain characters in the book.

C. He studies the pictures intently as you read the story.

5. Congratulations! Your child is learning the alphabet. During this crucial learning phase, he is most likely to practice his ABCs by:

A. Writing the alphabet.

B. Singing the alphabet.

C. Playing with letter-shaped blocks.

6. Your child has just solved a jigsaw puzzle and is very proud of herself. She is most likely to:

    A. Run and tell you about it.

    B. Call you in to show you the finished product.

    C. Take the puzzle apart so that you can watch her put it back together again.

7. Did you know that children laugh 146 times each day? That means your child laughs at a lot of things! But your child tends to laugh most at:

    A. Clowns and other slapstick comedians.

    B. Jokes or plays on words.

    C. Comic strips or cartoons.

8. During your child's alone time, he is most likely to:

    A. Watch TV.

    B. Play a game.

    C. Read a book or write a story.

9. There's nothing that warms a mother's heart like having her child say "I love you." Which of the following ways is your child most likely to show her love for you?

    A. The old fashioned way; by saying, "I love you."

    B. Drawing a beautiful picture of hearts and rainbows with the word "Mom" across it.

    C. Giving big hugs and kisses.

10. Every child has their own special talents. And your child seems to be most adept at:

    A. Music

B. Sports

C. Art

Now let's take a look at how you answered each of these questions and see which type of learning style best fits your child. Below is the answer to each question along with the type of learning style associated with each.

Question 1.
A. He'd watch the dog's every move intently—**Visual**
B. He'd immediately start petting the dog and engaging in a sort of play—**Kinesthetic**
C. He'd talk to the dog and try to communicate with it—**Auditory**

Question 2.
A. An active game—**Kinesthetic**
B. A fun word game—**Auditory**
C. A video game—**Visual**

Question 3.
A. Listen to you without budging—**Auditory**
B. Not be able to give you her full attention—**Kinesthetic**
C. Watch your lips moving and your gesticulations—**Visual**

Question 4.
A. You read the book to him out loud and take on interesting character voices—**Auditory**
B. He pretends to be certain characters in the book—**Kinesthetic**
C. He studies the pictures intently as you read the story—**Visual**

Question 5.
A. Writing the alphabet—**Visual**
 B. Singing the alphabet—**Auditory**
 C. Playing with letter-shaped blocks—**Kinesthetic**

Question 6.
A. Run and tell you about it—**Auditory**
B. Call you in to show you the finished product—**Visual**
C. Take the puzzle apart so that you can watch her put it
    back together again—**Kinesthetic**

Question 7.
A. Clowns and other slapstick comedians—**Kinesthetic**
B. Jokes or play-on-words - **Auditory**
C. Comic strips or cartoons—**Visual**

Question 8.
A. Watch TV—**Visual**
B. Play a game—**Kinesthetic**
C. Read a book or write a story—**Auditory**

Question 9.
A. The old fashioned way, saying "I love you"—**Auditory**
B. Drawing a beautiful picture of hearts and rainbows with
    the word "Mom" across it—**Visual**
C. Giving big hugs and kisses—**Kinesthetic**

Question 10.
A. Music—**Auditory**
B. Sports—**Kinesthetic**
C. Art—**Visual**

What Do These Results Mean?

Now that you can score your child on this quiz, what do these results mean and why is this important to you? First, I have to begin by saying that most individuals will not fit neatly into one of these styles. Your child will most likely have answers in at least two of these categories, if not all three; however, after reviewing the results, she will probably have a majority of her results in one of these areas. You can now use these results to teach to your child's strengths.

When teaching the tips I provide later on, you might have to tweak them to best fit your child's learning style. If your child is a visual learner, she might want to actually see real money and watch how you use it at the store. She might enjoy watching you interact when making a purchase or doing a transaction at the bank. If your child is an auditory learner, she might enjoy the talks you have with her about money. You could explain a budget to her and read money books that are geared towards children (I list some of these later on in the book). If your daughter is more of a kinesthetic learner, she would benefit from lessons in which she is actively involved in the process. She might enjoy using money to buy an item herself or counting out the money she earns dollar by dollar (or quarter by quarter).

This information is not given to make it harder for you to teach. I just want you to be aware of the unique ways that each of us learns and hopefully help you think of your child's unique learning strengths when teaching her about money. The most important thing is that you are reading this book, and you are eager to help your child start to gain an understanding of some basic financial principles.

CHAPTER 3
A Financial Literacy Quiz

*How Much Does My Child Already Know
About Money?*

To further illustrate the need to give our youth a financial education, I'd like to show you a quiz given in 2006 by Jump$tart.org. (I'm a teacher, so you just knew there would be some sort of test in this book, right?) This quiz was given to high school seniors to test their overall financial literacy. The results were not pretty, as the average score was 52.4%. If you have a high school student, I would like you to give this quiz to him. After the quiz, I have listed the correct answers to each question, the percentage of students who got each answer correct when tested by Jump$tart so that you can see how your child compares to a national average, and an explanation of the answer where needed. Get out your Number 2 pencils and let's get started—to make it easier, this is not a timed test:

1. If you have caused an accident, which type of automobile insurance would cover damage to your own car?
    A. Term
    B. Collision

C. Comprehensive

D. Liability

2. Matt and Eric are young men. Each has a good credit history. They work at the same company and make approximately the same salary. Matt has borrowed $6,000 to take a foreign vacation. Eric has borrowed $6,000 to buy a car. Who is least likely to pay the lowest finance charge?

  A. Matt will pay less because people who travel overseas are better risks.

  B. They will both pay the same because they have almost identical financial backgrounds.

  C. Eric will pay less because the car is collateral for the loan.

  D. They will both pay the same because the rate is set by law.

3. If you went to college and earned a 4-year degree, how much more money could you expect to earn than if you only had a high school diploma?

  A. A little more; about 20% more.

  B. A lot more; about 70% more.

  C. About 10 times as much.

  D. No more; I would make about the same either way.

4. Many savings programs are protected by the Federal Government against loss. Which of the following is not?

  A. A bond issued by one of the 50 States.

  B. A U.S. Treasury Bond.

C. A U.S. Savings Bond.

D. A certificate of deposit at the bank.

5. If each of the following persons had the same amount of take home pay, who would need the greatest amount of life insurance?

    A. A young single woman with two young children.

    B. A young single woman without children.

    C. An elderly retired man, with a wife who is also retired.

    D. A young married man without children.

6. Which of the following instruments is NOT typically associated with spending?

    A. Cash

    B. Credit Card

    C. Debit Card

    D. CD (Certificate of Deposit)

7. Which of the following credit card users is likely to pay the GREATEST dollar amount in finance charges per year if they all charge the same amount per year on their cards?

    A. Vera, who always pays off her credit card bill in full shortly after she receives it.

    B. Jessica, who only pays the minimum amount each month.

    C. Megan, who pays at least the minimum amount each month and more, when she has the money.

    D. Erin, who generally pays off her credit card in full but, occasionally, will pay the minimum when she is short of cash.

8. Which of the following statements is true?

  A. Your bad loan payment record with one bank will not be considered if you apply to another bank for a loan.

  B. If you missed a payment more than 2 years ago, it cannot be considered in a loan decision.

  C. Banks and other lenders share the credit history of their borrowers with each other and are likely to know of any loan payments that you have missed.

  D. People have so many loans it is very unlikely that one bank will know your history with another bank.

9. Doug must borrow $12,000 to complete his college education. Which of the following would NOT be likely to reduce the finance charge rate?

  A. If his parents took out an additional mortgage on their house for the loan.

  B. If the loan was insured by the Federal Government.

  C. If he went to a state college rather than a private collage.

  D. If his parents cosigned the loan.

10. If you had a savings account at a bank, which of the following would be correct concerning the interest that you would earn on this account?

  A. Sales tax may be charged on the interest that you earn.

  B. You cannot earn interest until you pass your 18th birthday.

C. Earnings from savings account interest may not be taxed.

D. Income tax may be charged on the interest if your income is high enough.

11. Inflation can cause difficulty in many ways. Which group would have the greatest problem during periods of high inflation that last several years?

A. Young couples with no children who both work.

B. Young working couples with children.

C. Older, working couples saving for retirement.

D. Older people living on a fixed income.

12. Which of the following is true about sales tax?

A. You don't have to pay the tax if your income is very low.

B. It makes things more expensive for you to buy.

C. The national sales tax percentage rate is 6%.

D. The federal government will deduct it from your paycheck.

13. Lindsay has saved $12,000 for her college expenses by working part-time. Her plan is to start college next year and she needs all of the money she saved. Which of the following is the safest place for her college money?

A. Corporate bonds

B. A bank savings account

C. Locked in her closet at home

D. Stocks

14. Which of the following types of investment would best protect the purchasing power of a family's savings in the event of a sudden increase in inflation?

A. A twenty-five year corporate bond

B. A house financed with a fixed-rate mortgage

C. A 10-year bond issued by a corporation

D. A certificate of deposit (CD) at a bank

15. Under which of the following circumstances would it be financially beneficial to you to borrow money to buy something now and repay it with future income?

    A. When some clothes you like go on sale.

    B. When the interest on the loan is greater than the interest you get on your savings.

    C. When you need to buy a car to get a much better paying job.

    D. When you really need a week vacation.

16. Which of the following statements best describes your right to check your credit history for accuracy?

    A. All credit records are the property of the U.S. Government and access is only available to the FBI and Lenders.

    B. You can only check your record for free if you are turned down for credit based on a credit report.

    C. Your credit record can be checked once a year for free.

    D. You cannot see your credit record.

17. Your take home pay from your job is less than the total amount you earn. Which of the following best describes what is taken out of your total pay?

    A. Federal income tax, social security and Medicare contributions

    B. Federal income tax, sales tax and social security contributions

C. Social security and Medicare contributions

D. Federal income tax, property tax, and Medicare and social security contributions

18. Retirement income paid by a company is called:
    A. Rents and profits
    B. Social Security
    C. 401k
    D. Pension

19. Many people put aside money to take care of unexpected expenses. If John and Jenny have money put aside for emergencies, in which of the following forms would it be of LEAST benefit to them if they needed it right away?
    A. Stocks
    B. Savings account
    C. Invested in a down payment on the house
    D. Checking account

20. Justin just found a job with a take-home pay of $2,000 per month. He must pay $800 for rent and $200 for groceries each month. He also spends $200 per month on transportation. If he budgets $100 each month for clothing, $150 for restaurants and $250 for everything else, how long will it take him to accumulate savings of $900?
    A. 1 month
    B. 2 months
    C. 3 months
    D. 4 months

21. Many young people receive health insurance benefits through their parents. Which of the following statements is true about health insurance coverage?
    A. Young people don't need health insurance because they are so healthy.
    B. You continue to be covered by your parents' insurance as long as you live at home, regardless of your age.
    C. You are covered by your parents' insurance until you marry, regardless of your age.
    D. If your parents become unemployed, your insurance coverage may stop, regardless of your age.

22. Mike and Dave work together in the finance department of the same company and earn the same pay. Mike spends his free time taking work-related classes to improve his computer skills while Dave spends his free time socializing with friends and working out at a fitness center. After five years, what is likely to be true?
    A. Mike will make more money because he is more valuable to his company.
    B. Mike and Dave will continue to make the same money.
    C. Dave will make more because he is more social.
    D. Dave will make more because Mike is likely to be laid off.

23. If your credit card is stolen and the thief runs up a total debt of $1,000 but you notify the issuer of the card as soon as you discover it is missing, what is the maximum amount that you can be forced to pay according to Federal law?

A. Nothing
B. $50
C. $500
D. $1,000

24. Which of the following statements is NOT correct about most ATM cards?
    A. You can get cash anywhere in the world with no fee.
    B. You must have a bank account to have an ATM card.
    C. You can generally get cash 24 hours a day.
    D. You can generally obtain information concerning your bank balance at an ATM machine.

25. Mark has a good job on the production line of a factory in his home town. During the past year or two, the state in which Mark lives has been raising taxes on its businesses to the point where they are much higher than in neighboring states. What effect is this likely to have on Mark's job?
    A. Mark's company may consider moving to a lower-tax state, threatening Mark's job.
    B. He is likely to get a large raise to offset the effect of higher taxes.
    C. Higher business taxes will cause more businesses to move into Mark's state, raising wages.
    D. Higher business taxes can't have any effect on Mark's job.

26. Kelly and Pete just had a baby. They received money as baby gifts and want to put it away for the baby's

education. Which of the following tends to have the highest growth over periods of time as long as 18 years?

    A. A U.S. Government Savings Bond

    B. A savings account

    C. A checking account

    D. Stocks

27. Karen has just applied for a credit card. She is an 18-year-old high school graduate with few valuable possessions and no credit history. If Karen is granted a credit card, which of the following is the most likely way that the credit card company will reduce its risk?

    A. It will charge Karen twice the finance charge rate it charges other cardholders.

    B. It will start Karen out with a small line of credit to see how she handles the account.

    C. It will make Karen's parents pledge their home to repay Karen's credit card debt.

    D. It will require Karen to have both parents co-sign for the card.

28. Maria worked her way through college earning $20,000 per year. After graduation, her first job pays $40,000 per year. The total dollar amount Maria will have to pay in Federal Income taxes in her new job will:

    A. Stay the same as when she was in college.

    B. Be lower than when she was in college.

    C. Double, at least, from when she was in college.

    D. Go up a little from when she was in college.

29. Which of the following best describes the primary sources of income for most people ages 20-35?

A. Profits from business

B. Rents

C. Dividends and interest

D. Salaries, wages, tips

30. If you are behind on your debt payments and go to a responsible credit counseling service such as the Consumer Credit Counseling Services, what help can they give you?

    A. They can work with those who loaned you money to set up a payment schedule that you can meet.

    B. They can force those who loaned you money to forgive all your debts.

    C. They can cancel and cut up all of your credit cards without your permission.

    D. They can get the Federal Government to apply your income taxes to pay off your debts.

ANSWER KEY

1. B. Collision

    50.5% got this answer correct

Collision insurance coverage pays for damage caused to your vehicle in an automobile accident, when **you are "at fault."** A standard collision automobile insurance policy will pay for any repairs up to the fair market value of your car. Collision coverage usually also comes with an **insurance deductible**. It's the amount of money you pay toward repairs before your collision insurance kicks in. The higher the deductible you're willing to pay, the **less the collision policy will cost**.

Comprehensive is very similar to collision insurance, the main difference being that comprehensive covers damage caused to your vehicle caused by any **unknown party** or **"act of God."** Vandalism, flood, hurricane, theft, and fire are all events usually covered by comprehensive automobile insurance. Like collision automobile insurance, comprehensive coverage will pay up to the fair market value of your car (less your insurance deductible.) And although it's not legally required by any state, you will probably need it if your car is financed.

Liability covers other people's bodily injuries or death for which you are responsible. It also provides for a legal defense if another party in the accident files a lawsuit against you. Claims for bodily injury may be for such things as medical bills, loss of income or pain and suffering. It also covers you if your car damages someone else's property. Usually it is their car, but it could be a fence, a house or any other property damaged in an accident. It also provides you with legal defense if another party files a lawsuit against you.

2. C. Eric will pay less because the car is collateral for the loan.

52.7% got this answer correct

Eric will pay less because the lender can go after his car as collateral for the loan. Matt's lender would have nothing to recover if Matt spent the money he borrowed on a vacation.

3. B. A lot more; about 70% more.

63.9% got this answer correct

We discuss the value of a college education later on.

4. A. A Bond issued by one of the 50 States.

28.6% got this answer correct

State bonds are not backed by the federal government.

5. A. A young single woman with two young children.

61.3% got this answer correct

If something tragic were to happen and this woman passed away, she would want the most life insurance to replace her income and take care of her children.

6. D. Certificate of deposit

93.5% got this answer correct

A certificate of deposit (or CD) is invested for a set period of time to earn interest.

7. B. Jessica, who only pays the minimum amount each month.

70.6% got this answer correct

Jessica is only paying the minimum amount on her credit card bill each month and will, thus, be carrying the most debt month to month. This will lead her to pay the most in interest charges

8. C. Banks and other lenders share the credit history of their borrowers with each other and are likely to know of any loan payments that you have missed.

70.9% got this answer correct

9. C. If he went to a state college rather than a private college.

30.4% got this answer correct

While state colleges are almost always cheaper to attend than private ones, the finance rate charged does not take which college one attends into consideration.

10. D. Income tax may be charged on the interest if your income is high enough.

22.7% got this answer correct

Interest on a bank savings account is taxable.

11. D. Older people living on fixed income retirement.

44.1% got this answer correct

If you are living on a set amount of money, increases in the cost of living make this amount pay for less.

12. B. It makes things more expensive for you to buy.

49.6% got this answer correct

When you buy something from a store this tax is added to the cost of the item which makes it more expensive for you to buy.

13. B. A bank savings account

80.4% got this answer correct

Since Lindsay's plan is to start college next year she would not want to tie her money up into bonds or risk investing it in stocks. She could lock it in her closet but a fire or burglary could wipe this out. A bank account would be her best bet since it would be backed by the federal government (FDIC insurance).

14. B. A house financed with a fixed-rate mortgage

44.6% got this answer correct

Housing values usually go up along with raises in the cost of living. In addition, in the case of inflation, you would be locked into a fixed-rate mortgage payment which would not increase. Bonds and CDs have set interest rates and would, thus, be worth less when they matured if sudden inflation were to occur.

15. C. When you need to buy a car to get a much better paying job.

 57.8% got this answer correct

If putting out money for a new car would guarantee you a higher-paying job, this would make financial sense because this purchase would pay for itself when you factor in the salary increase.

16. C. Your credit record can be checked once a year for free.

 50.1% got this answer correct

It is your right to receive a free copy of your credit record once annually from each of the credit reporting agencies.

17. A. Federal income tax, Social Security and Medicare contributions

 53% got this answer correct

Federal income taxes and Social Security and Medicare contributions are automatically deducted from your paycheck. If you live in a state that has an income tax, that will probably be automatically deducted, too.

18. D. Pension

 37.7% got this answer correct

Pension income is paid by a company to its employees who are retired and have worked enough years to earn a pension benefit. This used to be very common in many companies but the number of companies that now offer a pension has greatly decreased from years past. This is why it is important for you to take an active role in investing for your retirement.

19. C. Invested in a down payment on the house

 42.7% got this answer correct

Money put down on a house would be the slowest to access since it would be tied up in the house and not accessible until the house was sold (you could get a home equity loan which would, in a way, be like getting some of your down payment back). Even though stocks can be sold any day the financial markets are open, they would not be a good place to keep your emergency fund because the price might be down when you need to sell them to pay for something.

20. C. 3 months

66.3% got this answer correct

Justin's monthly expenses total $1,700. Subtract this from his $2,000 monthly income and that leaves him with $300. If Justin saved this $300 each month it would take him 3 months to have $900 saved.

21. D. If your parents become unemployed, your insurance coverage may stop, regardless of your age.

40.3% got this answer correct

If your parents lose a job that is providing their insurance (along with their child's), then the child would not be covered anymore.

22. A. Mike will make more money because he is more valuable to his company.

71.8% got this answer correct

This is pretty apparent. If you provide more value to your company, you will likely be compensated for this added value.

23. B. $50

15.1% got this answer correct

According to the Fair Credit Billing Act (FCBA), your

maximum liability under federal law for unauthorized use of your credit card is $50. If you report the loss before your credit cards are used, the FCBA says the card issuer cannot hold you responsible for any unauthorized charges. If a thief uses your cards before you report them missing, the most you will owe for unauthorized charges is $50 per card. Also, if the loss involves your credit card number, but not the card itself, you have no liability for unauthorized use.

24. A. You can get cash anywhere in the world with no fee.
    66.8% got this answer correct
    Many banks charge fees for taking money out at another bank's ATM machine. Some of these can be as high as $5 when all is said and done.

25. A. Mark's company may consider moving to a lower-tax state, threatening Mark's job.
    59.0% got this answer correct
    This is pretty easy to understand. Most companies are in business to ultimately make money. If they can move to a location where they have to pay less, most will jump at this opportunity.

26. D. Stocks
    14.2% got this answer correct
    Stocks have the best long-term returns (around 10% average growth per year) by far, easily beating bonds and savings accounts.

27. B. It will start Karen out with a small line of credit to see how she handles the account.
    55.3% got this answer correct

This used to be the only correct answer but the Credit Card Reform Act that became effective on February 22, 2010, changed this somewhat. According to this act, if you are under 21, you will need to show that you are able to make payments, or you will need a cosigner, in order to open a credit card account. If you are under age 21 and have a card with a cosigner and want an increase in the credit limit, your cosigner must agree in writing to the increase.

28. C. Double, at least, from when she was in college.
     42.1% got this answer correct
This will depend on her new income tax bracket but the amount she will pay in taxes will increase greatly.

29. D. Salaries, wages, tips
     77.8% got this answer correct
While someone in this bracket could earn income from all of the choices, the most likely way someone in this bracket would earn money is through their place of employment.

30. A. They can work with those who loaned you money to set up a payment schedule that you can meet.
     67.1% got this answer correct
This is the only choice a counseling service could offer you to help you pay off your debt.

Don't fret if your child (or you for that matter) did not ace this test. That is the reason you are reading this book—to better educate yourself and pass this knowledge on to your child.

Section 3

Teaching To The Student/Narrowing The Scope

The next six chapters are broken down into age brackets and activities you can use to teach your child about money depending on his/her age.

As a classroom teacher, I would not expect a kindergarten student to acquire the same knowledge that a 5th grader could. The same holds true with teaching your child about money. Older children can usually be taught different concepts with more complexity than younger students. Since this is the case, I have divided the chapters into the following age groups:

Ages 3 – 5
Ages 6 – 8
Ages 9 – 11
Ages 12 – 14
Ages 15 – 18
Ages 19 and Up

There is a reason for this grouping. Children ages 3–5 are in the pre-school range and have shorter attention spans, and thus, the activities taught to them need to be direct and hands-on. Children ages 6–8 are usually in kindergarten–second grade and are referred to as being in a primary grade. You can expand on the lessons they were taught when they were younger but still cannot go too deep. The next bracket (ages

9–11) makes up the secondary grades in elementary school, grades 3–5. These children can be taught more in-depth lessons, reviewing some of the previously-taught concepts with more explanation. Following this bracket are 12–14-year-olds, the middle school years. This is really when you can see the lessons you teach sink in. Many children in this age bracket have a good understanding of what money is and its uses, and thus, you can begin talking about more mature topics.

The next chapter discusses ideas to use with your high school student. Children in this age bracket (ages 15–18) may already know quite a bit about money because they work or are starting to learn about the student loan process while they apply to college. The final age bracket is for the young adult years. Although it may be hard to believe, once your child reaches this age, she is no longer a kid. This is the "welcome to the real world" chapter and gives advice to reach those who are now realizing how important money really is.

I know these chapters are categorized according to age, but you do have the flexibility to teach the lessons in each depending on the needs of your child. For instance, if your child is 15 but has very limited knowledge of money, you may want to start in an earlier chapter to build up her knowledge. On the flip side, your child may be 6 but already understands many of the concepts discussed in the chapter corresponding to her age. If this is the case (first, congratulations are in order), move up to the next chapter and discuss some of the concepts taught there. The chapters are meant to be a guideline for you and not something that you have to follow exactly.

So that you can have a heads-up and start preparing to teach your child, here are some of the concepts and topics that will be introduced in the next 6 chapters:

✓ Creating a chore chart and what to teach your child with the money earned from doing chores

✓ Needs and wants

✓ How going above and beyond others pays off

✓ Student loans

✓ Credit cards

✓ Finding your sweet spot

✓ Working outside the home

✓ The Emergency Fund

✓ Budgeting

✓ The borrower is servant to the lender (debt)

✓ The magic of compound interest

✓ The value of work

✓ Debit card

✓ Freedom with large expenses

✓ Establishing long-term goals

✓ Teach by not saving the day!

✓ Leading by example

✓ Self-control

✓ Is it truly a need

✓ The value of work

✓ Looking at any job as an opportunity

✓ Potential jobs for teens

✓ Tips for preparing for a job interview

✓ Common questions to expect on a job interview along with potential answers to these questions

✓ Balancing a checkbook

- ✓ Uncle Sam—Why are taxes taken out and what do they pay for
- ✓ Bank accounts
- ✓ Saving and investing for the future—The magic of compound interest
- ✓ Paying for college
- ✓ Life after school
- ✓ Is college the best option for all
- ✓ The gap year
- ✓ Freedom
- ✓ Finding your purpose
- ✓ Does money guarantee happiness
- ✓ Placing a value on money
- ✓ Post college job search
- ✓ The married life
- ✓ Health insurance
- ✓ Buying a house
- ✓ Turning lemons into lemonade—Examples of people who have done this
- ✓ Embracing failure—Examples of people who overcame failure to achieve greatness
- ✓ Quotes about failure
- ✓ College is not the end of the road

Now that you have an idea of the concepts and ideas we will discuss, let's get going—your child's future may depend on how well you teach these important concepts to her.

CHAPTER 4
Pre-School Years
Ages 3–5

*It Is Never Too Early To Discuss Money With
A Child (Even A 3-Year-Old!)*

The pre-school years, ages three to five, are when children are first starting to have some curiosity about money. They see you buy things by giving the cashier some green bills or by swiping a piece of plastic through a machine. Many experiences are completely new to them and *this* is the time you can start to discuss and help them develop sound financial principles that will have an impact on them for the rest of their lives. I know many might feel that starting at age three is way too young to talk about money, but after reading this chapter, I hope you will see that it is never too early, and even little ones are eager to learn.

The Exchange – You Need Money To Buy Things

When children are at pre-school age, they will notice that when you purchase something you either have to hand over cash or swipe your debit/credit card in a machine. They will often wonder and ask why you are doing this—here is your opportunity to teach them their first money lesson.

I would encourage you to use cash when teaching this lesson since it will be a more concrete example to use rather than trying to explain how a debit/credit card works. Your child can see that when you hand over a certain amount, you get an item in return. You can show them that we use cash as a means of exchange.

Explain to them what cash and coins are and let them hold money, look at it and ask questions about who is on it (added bonus—a little history lesson, too). Help them learn how to identify a penny, a nickel, a dime and a quarter, and know the value of each of these. You do not have to go into great detail at this point; you are simply trying to help them understand that everything you buy has a certain price placed on it.

Discuss with children items they enjoy. These might include eating ice cream, watching television, playing on the computer, etc. Each of these cost money. This is a great time for them to have a basic understanding that many of the things we enjoy have a price attached to them. On the flip side, discuss some enjoyable activities that do not cost anything. These may include playing with a friend or going for a nature walk. The goal is for your child to start developing a basic understanding of the purpose of money and what it can be used for.

Money Doesn't Grow On Trees – How We Earn Money

After your child watches you exchange cash for something, you can extend her learning and tell her how you earned this cash. Many children at this age have an idea that you go to work and maybe even know what your occupation is but cannot fully grasp why you work. After viewing a real-life transaction, extend the lesson a bit and ask your child if she knows how you got the cash needed to make the purchase she witnessed—be prepared to be entertained since we never know what will come out of the mouths of babes. After your child has answered, you can explain that you earned this money by working. In exchange for your labor, you were paid a certain amount of money. You do not have to get too technical in this discussion. The important thing is that your child starts to understand the relationship between work and money.

The Chore Chart – Teaching The Uses Of Money

I feel that children start learning at an early age how money can be used. After my oldest daughter, Ava, turned three, we had her doing simple household chores so that we could teach her how to handle money. I first must begin by saying that I am not a fan of rewarding children for things they *should be* doing. I did, however, make an exception with Ava since my initial goal was to teach her money management skills. We started with chores which were easy for her to complete: cleaning her room, brushing her teeth, and so on. Every night we would check off the chores completed, and every Friday we added them up and she was paid. We called this money what most parents do: an allowance. There are other parents who feel it should be called a commission or such, since one has to produce to get paid. No matter what you call it, make sure your child does the work to earn the money.

After Ava got paid (she could earn up to $1 each week), she had three jars: one labeled Give Away, one Savings and the other Spending. She first put 10 cents in the Give Away jar, 25 cents in the Savings jar and the remaining amount in the Spending jar. This worked so well for us. When we were at the store, often Ava would see something she wanted. We never had any arguments; we would simply say, "We'll have to go home and see if you have enough money in your spending and/or savings jar to buy it."

Ava has used the money in her Give Away jar in numerous ways. One year there was a little girl at my school who lost her father shortly before Christmas. Ava used her Give Away money to buy this little girl a stuffed animal. Ava actually came to my school and delivered this to her personally. Another year, Ava used this money to buy canned food for needy families in our community. One Christmas, there was a family at her school that was struggling financially. Ava used the money in her Give Away jar to buy them a gift card to a local grocery store.

Ava uses the money in her Savings jar to buy things that cost a few weeks' worth of allowance. We let her use her Spending jar for anything she wants. Sometimes I have to bite my tongue because some of the things she buys are junk. I refrain from saying anything because I would rather her make mistakes now and only blow a couple of bucks than wait until she is older when those same mistakes may be much more costly.

Ava has shown me that these lessons in money management are paying off. Twice a year the media center at her school hosts a book fair. The children get very excited and want to buy almost everything they see—it's almost like Black Friday for kids. When Ava was in kindergarten, she came home after visiting the book fair and had to have a Taylor Swift book. Now, with her mom and dad both being former first-grade teachers, she probably has 2,000 books. It was hard for me not to say anything but we looked in her Savings jar and she had enough for this book—$5. The next day she brought her money to school to purchase it. When she got home that afternoon, she still had the $5 in her backpack. We asked why she didn't buy the book and Ava told us that it had sold out and was no longer for sale. I was shocked—most kids (and adults, too) would have that money burn a hole in their pocket and would've moved on and bought something else. Here's where the story gets really good. The next day, the media specialist called and said they had found some more copies of this book. She told me she would set one aside for Ava. Later that day, I told Ava the good news. She was thrilled. It was a wonderful learning opportunity for Ava. I told her many people would have spent their money on something they didn't really want, and when the item they originally were going to buy became available, they wouldn't be able to purchase it. This situation showed me that some of what I was teaching Ava was, in fact, sinking in.

A Nintendo DS – Wants vs. Needs

I feel that you can also discuss the concept of Wants versus Need once your child turns five, and use concrete examples to better explain this.

When Ava was five, she really wanted a Nintendo DS for Christmas. Tracy and I didn't have this in our Christmas budget. Even though I'm pretty frugal I have to admit that I thought hard about buying this for her. After all, Christmas only comes once a year and she was a good girl and she didn't want a lot of other things and she was doing well in school and . . . I could go on and on with reasons she should have a DS and justify buying it for her. Tracy and I finally sat down to really discuss it and came to the conclusion that since it exceeded the amount we had set aside for Christmas spending, the DS would have to wait for later. Christmas came and went and Ava enjoyed all of the gifts she received. She did mention that maybe she could get a DS for her birthday but that was it. She was not devastated and will not need counseling because she did not receive this present.

The very Sunday after Christmas, our heat went out and we had to have someone come and repair our unit. The interesting thing is that the bill was a little over the amount we would have spent on a DS. How weird is that? I then used this as a teaching opportunity, explaining to Ava why we have an emergency fund set up and how we don't use this money for wants—like a Nintendo DS.

Summary

I know that these ages seem a little early to start teaching children about money but I feel the little examples mentioned here can help prepare your child for the years ahead. The goal when they are this young is to get them to understand the basics of money. Let them see what actual money looks like—with the use of credit and debit cards this may be a foreign concept to some of you.

In this chapter we discussed the following financial concepts that you can introduce to your child:

✓ The Exchange – You Need Money To Buy Things
✓ Money Doesn't Grow On Trees – How We Earn Money

✓ The Chore Chart – Teaching The Uses Of Money

✓ A Nintendo DS – Wants vs. Needs

While it is true that many lessons you teach your children in this age group may seem too advanced and way over their heads, you would be surprised at how much they are listening and what is actually sinking in. Do not become too discouraged if your child does not seem to grasp each concept or show any interest in them. These are the beginning stages of laying a solid financial foundation.

CHAPTER 5

Primary Years
Ages 6–8

When Kids Become Sponges And Are Ready
To Soak Up Knowledge

I feel that once a child turns six, you can start to explain money issues in a more complex way. For example, I started showing Ava the list of our expenses I paid out of my check. I discussed how I had to pay for the mortgage, electric, food and the other necessities. I wanted her to get an understanding that when I tell her we are not buying something she wants (this happens more and more as they reach this age) it is not because I am the meanest dad ever—it is because I have other priorities I need to pay for first.

Many parents think this type of talk is above their child's head, but have you ever sat down and played a video game with a young person? Most can figure out what the buttons on the remote do in about five minutes while I am still lost an hour later. Kids are like sponges at this age—they are ready to soak up knowledge like a sponge does water.

A topic that can be re-introduced at ages six to eight is that we need money to buy things. Most of us have a limited amount of money, and thus, have to budget accordingly. Help your child learn this by having him help you create the weekly grocery list. Explain that you have a set amount of money to spend on food and let him help you plan this list according to your budget. To make this fun, have him look through the Sunday paper and clip any coupons that will help save money. As an added bonus, pay him the money he helped you save by using coupons. You get to kill two birds with one stone doing this—your child gets actively involved in this process and receives a financial reward that did not cost you a cent because it was money that would have been spent without his help in finding the coupons.

Another great discussion to have at this point is to let your child know (or remind him of what they have previously learned) that you earn this grocery money by working. Describe your job to your child and let him know exactly what you do. In addition, while out in your city, point out other people who are working—police officers, cashiers and even his teacher. Point out others who have started their own business as their occupations. This could be your favorite mom and pop restaurant or maybe a local toy store. Explain to your child that these people are known as entrepreneurs. To get his creative juices flowing, encourage him to think of some ways he could work to earn money. Maybe something like starting a lemonade stand or walking a neighbor's dog. This is meant to show him that there are a variety of jobs and ways to make money.

Now is also an ideal time to discuss the difference between

wants and needs. When you are out shopping with your child, point out the essentials such as food and clothing and ask him why these things are needs. Then ask him to describe some items he may want but are optional. Discuss how you decide what to buy and what to pass up. You could ask, "What is more important, buying food or a video game?" Since your child is more mature, you can go into a more detailed conversation concerning this topic than we did in the previous chapter.

With the topic of wants and needs you can also bring up why you have to wait before buying something. You can even get into the pitfalls of using credit cards (usually used to purchase items we do not currently have the money to buy) and how this can lead to financial ruin. Discuss with your child how he sometimes has to wait for his turn to swing at school or how he always has to wait for his favorite holiday or birthday to come around and that this is what makes these days so special—they only come once a year. The same concept holds true when we save up before buying something. Because we have sacrificed and saved, this item usually means much more to us.

Scrubbing Toilets – Going Above and Beyond Pays Off

In the previous chapter, I showed how I started having my daughter, Ava, do chores and how she was paid for these. When Ava turned six, I changed the way she was paid and how she was able to earn her allowance. I explained to her that the chores she once got paid for doing were now actions she was expected to do as a member of our family. The upside was she could now get a raise and earn $1.50 each week. To earn this money, she would have to gather the garbage around the house every Sunday and clean her bathroom—this included cleaning her mirror and sink and scrubbing the toilet—once a week. Now that she had a basic understanding of money management, I wanted to teach her that going above and beyond can pay off (I am fairly certain that not many six-year-olds scrub their toilets.) I feel if Ava continues to apply these lessons in life—gives away 10% of her money, then saves 25% of it and uses the remainder for spending (the jars we discussed in the last chapter)—and goes above and beyond in her job, she will be wealthy in more ways than one.

Free Money – Opening A Bank Account

By the time Ava had turned eight, she had a decent amount of money in her Savings and Spending jars. I told her there was a better place to put this money—in a bank.

I discussed a few reasons why a bank account was a safer place for her money rather than a plastic container. These included a fire (God forbid), theft or just plain misplacing it. I then mentioned the best reason to place her money in a savings account—she would be "paid" by the bank for doing this.

I know the interest is not great with many banks, but earning even $1 a year in interest can be pretty big for an eight-year-old. Investing is something we will introduce at a later age, but for now I wanted her to see the importance of placing her savings (or emergency fund) in a bank rather than just have it sit around the house.

It just so happened that around this time a local bank was offering to match up to $50 when a child opened a savings account at their branch. Ava had $192 and I told her if she opened an account at this bank, her $192 would turn into

$242 just like that (she did have to keep this account for 90 days for this reward to kick in)! This was pretty powerful for her and her eyes grew very wide. I briefly explained why the bank would do this but did not need to convince her at all— I had her at hello (or at least free money).

It just so happened that we took this trip to the bank about a week after we played Monopoly and she lost all she had (more on this in the next chapter). Since I knew this game was still fresh in her mind, I decided to tie it into her savings account. I asked to her to think back to our game and how I seemed to have nothing but good luck towards the end, when I had many properties that she kept landing on. I told her that it seemed like I kept getting richer and richer and how this is often true in life as well. I then brought up her new savings account. Some of her friends who did not have money to deposit may think it was not fair that she got $50 for free just by opening this account. I then explained that she put herself in this position because she chose to save her money and not buy the latest and greatest toy or video game. She made some sacrifices and took actions that her friends did not. I went on to explain that many people who have a lot of money were able to put themselves in the position to make more money by planning ahead and making some sacrifices. Like the old saying goes—"Good things come to those who wait."

On The Way To School – Student Loans

In addition to the lessons you can teach using chores and allowance, you can also begin to discuss more grown-up financial matters with your child. In fact, you could start a basic discussion about student loans.

During the last week of Ava's first-grade year, her school had an Awards Day for the students. Ava got a gold medal (it was real gold according to her) for exceeding in all academic areas. Not many of her peers obtained this so I was very proud of her for working so hard at school. The next morning, on our way to school, I told Ava how proud I was of her and started to discuss the importance of getting good grades and giving her best effort. I know college is far off but it will be here before we know it. I told Ava that if she continues to do well until she graduates from high school, she will have more options on where she can go to college. I also told her that a college might even pay for her to attend their school. Ava then said, "That's called a scholarship." My mouth about dropped to the floor—we were on to something here. I then went further and explained that if she did not get a scholarship she could still go to college but would probably have to work or get a student loan.

Tracy and I do invest for both our daughters' college, but may not have enough to cover the entire tuition ourselves. I went on to tell her that once she graduates and gets a job, she will have to start paying this loan off. Ava then said, "I will actually have to pay more than the amount the loan was for." Now I was really in shock. I asked her how she knew this and she replied, "Most people don't just give you money for free —you have to pay them more since they let you borrow it." At this point I did not know what to say. My seven-year-old knows more about student loans than many college freshmen do. When I got to school, I called Tracy to let her know about our conversation. It turns out, Ava and Tracy had had a similar conversation the day before. This just shows how much our kids are listening and what they remember.

A Visit To The Dentist – Credit Cards

Another grown-up topic you can discuss with your child is credit card debt. I drive Ava to school most mornings (that is a plus of being a teacher). One morning, Tracy was taking Ella, our then 3-year-old daughter, to the dentist during the day. On the way out the door to school, I told Tracy to use the credit card to pay. When we got into my car, Ava said, "I thought credit cards were bad to use, Dad." You can tell whose daughter she is, huh? Whenever such an opportunity arises, I make sure to use it as a teaching example.

I explained to her that yes, for many, credit cards are not wise to use. A lot of people use them without having the money to pay the balance off in full each month. I then told Ava that Tracy and I have two accounts at the bank—a checking account and a savings account. I have divided the money we have in our savings account into different categories including medical (other categories include expenses I know will come out during the year including car insurance, Christmas and vacation). I went on and explained that I get paid once a month, and instead of constantly transferring money from our savings to our checking account, Tracy and I keep track of what we put on our credit card—this is written down on a post-it note that is in our check register—and just transfer this entire amount over at the end of the month to payoff our credit card in full.

I pointed out to Ava that the most important point is we know we have the money to pay for anything we purchase on our credit card. People who buy things knowing they don't actually have the money to pay for them usually end up in trouble. Ava then showed me that she understood how important this was by saying the following, "Dad, those people who don't pay off their credit cards each month can lose their house." Wow, pretty deep for a seven-year-old.

Once again, this conversation was a reminder that our kids are listening more than we think and understand a lot more than we give them credit for. Yes, Ava may have been stretching it a little bit by thinking that anyone who does not pay off their credit card each month will eventually lose their home; however, I was not about to correct her. I would love for her to continue to think this way. If she continues this line of thinking, she will hopefully never buy something she doesn't have the money for because the fear of losing her home will come to mind. I would much rather her be wrong in this assumption than buy things she cannot afford. You see, if she does the former she may one day lose her home. If she does the latter, the odds of that happening are slim to none!

The Christmas Wish List – Wants vs. Needs

During this time, you can also re-visit the topic of Wants versus Needs. Around Christmas, Nielsen recently conducted a survey among children between the ages of 6 and 12 asking what was on their list for Santa. Unless you own stock in Apple, you might not like the findings. Here is that list followed by the percentage of children who wanted each item:

iPad: 44%
iPod Touch: 30%
iPhone: 27%
Computer: 25%
Tablet Computer (non iPad): 25%
Nintendo 3DS: 25%
Kinect for Xbox 360: 23%
Nintendo DS/DSi/DS Lite: 22%

Television Set: 20%
Smartphone (non iPhone): 19%
Sony PlayStation 3/PS3 Slim: 17%
Blu-Ray Player: 17%
E-Reader: 17%
Xbox 360: 16%
Other Mobile Phone: 12%
Nintendo Wi: 11%
PlayStation Move: 10%
PlayStation Portable: 10%

While it takes a minute for your mouth to close, here is a sampling of some of the prices of the above-listed items:

iPad: $499 (this is the price they start at)
iPod Touch: $189
Nintendo 3DS: $189
Blu-Ray Player: $68
Nintendo Wi: $179

I enjoy reading surveys but surely this would not correlate to what my then seven-year-old would want for Christmas. I mean, she has been raised by pretty frugal parents and we discuss money issues all the time with her. In fact, she has a better understanding than many teenagers I know.

Shortly after Thanksgiving we had Ava make her list for Santa Claus. Well, once again I was wrong. The number one item on her list was an iPod Touch!! Really? Whatever happened to Barbie Dolls and Tinker Toys? How about Legos or some clothes? An iPod Touch for a seven-year-old? I am 38 and have a job and don't even own one of these. I was not this dramatic in my response to her but it really opened my eyes. Like I mentioned, we are a pretty frugal family and discuss money-related issues with our children on a consistent basis. Even though this is true, Ava still wanted one of these more expensive gifts.

I know many parents are still struggling with the recent economic downturn so we have to be very careful on how we are spending money. It is very easy to get caught up in the holiday rush and buy things you cannot afford—especially when it comes to your children. Most parents want their child(ren) to have a magical Christmas morning they will remember forever. The truth is, your son will probably not even remember what he got this year once next Christmas rolls around (go ahead and see if you can name every gift you got last Christmas—I know I can't). I would have loved for Ava to wake up and be so happy that she got what she wanted from Santa but we did not have that amount of money budgeted for Christmas that year. Even though I could come up with reasons that she "deserved" an iPod Touch, I was not willing to dip into my emergency fund to buy it for her. Although she did not get this gift, I am sure she will not need to go on *The Dr. Phil Show* for counseling. She did not seem too disappointed, but even if she was, life went on and she still had a Merry Christmas.

A Money Conversion Game

In the next chapter we are going to explore how playing Monopoly with your child can lead to some great discussion and help you teach him a valuable lesson. To further enhance your child's learning, here is another game you can play with him.

You can adjust the complexity of this game depending on your child's knowledge level. If he is six years old, you will probably just work on counting pennies and converting these coins into nickels. If your child is more advanced, play up to accumulating $1 (or you could go higher if you wish—use your own parental discretion).

To begin, you need a die, a sheet of paper and 10 pennies, 4 nickels, 6 dimes, 8 quarters and a $1 bill. In level 1, we are going to see who gets five pennies first. Each person takes turns rolling the die and collecting the number of pennies they roll. If you or your child rolls a 2, 4 or a 6, they collect 2 pennies. If you roll a 1, 3 or 5, collect 1 penny. If you have a die that just has a 1, 2 and 3 on it, that would be ideal. However, most of us do not have this type so we can make accommodations using a regular one. The player who gets to five pennies first wins.

In Level 2, we are going to see who gets two nickels first. Get a sheet of paper and divide it in half with a marker. Label one side pennies and the other nickels. Take turns rolling the die (if you want, you can now collect the number of pennies you actually roll). When a player gets five pennies, he must convert them to a nickel by removing five pennies from the pennies side of the paper and placing a nickel on the nickel side. The first person to collect two nickels (or however many you want to play to) wins the game.

In the next level you will see who gets 3 dimes (or however many you choose) first. Divide a sheet of paper into thirds— one-third is labeled pennies, one nickels and the other dimes. Take turns rolling the die. As in level 2, when a player gets 5 pennies, he must convert them to a nickel. Now, when a person gets two nickels, he must convert them into a dime. The first player to get three dimes (or however many you choose) wins.

The next level may be the most difficult one to teach to

your child because he will have to pull from two rows to make a quarter (has to pull 1 nickel and 2 dimes). Divide a piece of paper into fourths—label these fourths pennies, nickels, dimes and quarters. Follow the directions from the previous levels but when your child gets two dimes and one nickel, she has to convert these three coins to a quarter. The first person to get two quarters wins.

In the last level, the first person to exchange 4 quarters for the $1 bill wins. Use the same rules as in the previous levels, but when a person collects 4 quarters, he can convert them to the $1 bill and wins the game. This is a fun way to teach your child coin recognition, the value of coins and how these coins can be converted when you have a certain number of each.

Summary

We discuss money topics with our children as often as we can. We talk openly about how much I make and the bills we have. I know some of the things we talk about are over our daughters' heads, but some of these conversations showed me that maybe they actually understand more than what I think they do. As a teacher, I know we don't teach enough financial skills to our students. If you are a parent it is so important to discuss money with your child(ren) when the opportunity presents itself—you never know the impact it will have on their future.

Some of the topics we addressed in this chapter include:

✓ Going Above and Beyond Pays Off – Scrubbing Toilets
✓ Opening A Bank Account – Free Money

✓ Student Loans – On The Way To School

✓ Credit Cards – A Visit To The Dentist

✓ Wants vs. Needs – The Christmas Wish List

Like in the previous chapter, some of these concepts may seem way above your child's comprehension. I hope you can now see how children in this age bracket think, and that they can understand many financial concepts we think they could not grasp. Even if you are discussing concepts which are a little above them, that is fine. I would rather you make the mistake (if you want to call it that) and share too much information than do the opposite and not share enough.

CHAPTER 6

Secondary Years
Ages 9–11

Make Your Child Smarter Than A 5th Grader
(At Least When It Come To Money)

The secondary years, ages nine to eleven, can be a hard adjustment for some. Once your child enters third grade, more is expected of her. Many states start giving standardized tests for students once they enter this grade and, thus, the stakes are much higher. Many become more aware of what is going on around them—this seems to have accelerated with the advent of technology. They are moving past the innocence of being young and may start to experience real-world issues such as making and maintaining friendships. In addition, many schools have the PE Coach and/or counselor give students The Talk—many of you know what I mean—in 4th and 5th grades. This can open up a world of questions. Even though it can be tough to see your baby grow up, this is also a great time to discuss more mature money (and other) matters) with her.

Peer pressure really starts to begin during these years. Since your child is more aware of her surroundings, she will notice what her peers are wearing and buying. This sparks a natural interest in learning more about money. This is your opportunity to begin to help your child establish healthy money values because if you don't, there are some eager teachers out there waiting to educate her—her real-life friends and those she watches on TV.

The Sweet Spot (Find This And You Will Never Feel Like You Are Working)

When Ava was in 4th grade, she tried out for and made the Reading Bowl Team at school. This was a huge accomplishment as only seven students made the team! They did really well in numerous competitions and actually made it to the state championship. The night before the state final, Ava and I were lying on her bed and talking. There was another student on the team who had demanding parents and Ava asked me if I would ever push her that hard. I told her that as long as she gave her best effort, I would not.

I then talked to her about finding her sweet spot in life. For you former (or current) baseball players out there, the sweet spot on a baseball bat is about 5-7 inches from the end of the barrel. When the batter hits the ball in this spot it seems to just fly off the bat and travel much farther than when it is struck elsewhere. In life, we also have a sweet spot. My good friend and radio show host Ken Coleman best explains life's sweet spot as follows:

Most people never truly find their sweet spot, the intersection of their greatest strength and their greatest passion. I am troubled by the epidemic of men and women who are good at their job but hate it. This is misery. Conversely, we all know people who love what they are doing but are not very good at it. This is frustration. The most successful among us find their sweet spot and stay there. This is fulfillment. We should spend all of our energy finding our sweet spot, the right place for us. When we get in the right place, opportunity, the right time, will find us.

I went on to discuss what finding your sweet spot may look like. In my case, my sweet spot is in helping others manage money. However, at this point, that alone cannot pay my bills so I am a school teacher as well. Many of us find ourselves in this situation—where our passions and talents alone do not enable us to pay all of our bills. I think of local bands whose members have day jobs to allow them to hit their sweet spots at night while playing at various venues. I told Ava that while I will always expect her to give her best effort in anything she tries, I would never push her to the point of making her want to quit. Once you hit that sweet spot, you will not need any encouragement.

Working Outside The Home (Finding Ways To Earn Money Other Than An Allowance)

From reading the last two chapters, you know that I am all for a child earning money by doing chores around the house. However, as parents, the goal is to teach our children sound money habits and practices so they will be able to support themselves as they enter adulthood. Believe it or not, children in this age range, from 9 to 11, can actually start earning money outside the house.

First, think about some of the strengths your child possesses. It may be she can fix broken toys or is a whiz with electronics and can create her own app. Many children have strengths that can help others.

An example of this is a young boy named Caine Monroy. I personally watched him present last year at the Chick-fil-A Leadercast event in Atlanta. When Caine was nine years old, he spent his summer vacation building an elaborate cardboard arcade inside his dad's used auto parts store. Whenever his dad had a customer, Caine would ask him to play one of his games. The entire summer went by, and despite his efforts, Caine had yet to have a single customer. One day a filmmaker named Nirvan Mullick stopped to buy a door handle for his car and became Caine's first customer. After playing at Caine's Arcade, Nirvan created and posted a video about his experience. What happened next was pure magic.

In less than one year after the video was posted the following happened:

- More than $231,000 had been raised for Caine's Scholarship Fund thanks to over 19,000 individual donors.

- More than 7 million views on YouTube and Vimeo.

- Caine and Nirvan launched the Imagination Foundation and their first annual Global Cardboard Challenge with more than 270 events in 41 countries engaging tens of thousands of kids worldwide in creative play.

- Caine was the youngest ever entrepreneur to speak at USC Marshall School of Business, Cannes Lions International Festival of Creativity, and even spoke at TEDxTeen hosted by Chelsea Clinton. Caine also received the Latino Spirit Award from the California State Assembly, and a cardboard key to the city.

• Thousands of people visited Caine's Arcade!

To learn more about Caine and his amazing story please visit http://cainesarcade.com.

Now I realize that Caine's story is pretty remarkable and not all children will be able to accomplish what he did; but I do feel that many have something to offer others. Ava is a pretty gifted writer. She has a unique voice in her samples and actually won the 2nd grade author of the year award for our entire county a few years ago. Since I had written a few books, and had some contacts in the publishing industry, I asked if she wanted to write a book and see if she could get it published. I explained this would be a way for her to share her gift with others and, at the same time, possibly earn some money (the money part is what intrigued her the most). Though her first book about vampires was not accepted, during Christmas break Ava worked on her second book idea about money lessons and Wyatt-MacKenzie Publishing accepted her book and it will be published!

I bet you could come up with some unique skills your child has that could potentially help others. Even if what they create does not make any money, it is still a great experience for your child in helping her start thinking about her talents and how this can lead to financial success.

Opening Doors (The Emergency Fund)

I have always stressed the importance of establishing an emergency fund to prepare for those things that will happen. If you live in a house long enough, you will eventually need a new roof. If you drive a car long enough, it will require repairs at some point. Being prepared can turn these events into inconveniences instead of catastrophes. In addition to preparing for emergencies, an emergency fund gives you margin to pursue unforeseen opportunities which could come your way.

While Ava was writing her book, I explained to her how I came to write my first book. In 2005, I had no intentions of ever becoming an author. I feel that one day God spoke to me and wanted me to get my thoughts on paper. After a few months of turning my thoughts into words, my "book" was complete. At this point, I was just pleased to have my words on paper to show family and friends. Someone suggested I try to get it published. Now, at this point, the publishing industry was completely different than it is now. I did get an offer to have my words turned into a book but I would have to pay almost $4,000 to make this happen. Now, this was not an emergency, but an opportunity.

Since Tracy and I had more than a fully established emergency fund (3-6 months of living expenses) we discussed and prayed about this opportunity. We did decide to have it published and a year later *How To Survive (and perhaps thrive) On A Teacher's Salary* was released. Fast forward to today and many wonderful things have happened because I was able to take advantage of this opportunity. In addition to the book you are currently reading, I have also published another one, *A Simple Book Of Financial Wisdom: Teach Yourself (and your kids) How To Live Wealthy On Little Money*. And I have another book coming out in the near future. These books have also given me the opportunity to appear on national television more than thirty times and be interviewed on more than 400 radio shows. There are numerous doors that have been opened for me because I had enough money saved to be able to take advantage of that initial publishing opportunity. In fact, Ava may not have been given the chance to publish her book if I was not prepared. I explained to her that having savings cannot only open doors for her, but for others as well.

Time On Electronics (Budgeting)

I don't know about your children but mine seem to love most of their electronic devices. While I think most of these devices can provide great learning activities, they need to be used in moderation. A way to teach about budgeting time is to give your child a certain number of hours a week she can spend on electronic devices. Just like with money, if she blows most of her time those first few days, she will have less time to spend on them the rest of the week. You can use this with other activities, too. The important thing is to teach your child that she has a set amount time and she needs to budget accordingly.

Monopoly Money – The Borrower Is Servant To The Lender (Debt)

I used to enjoy playing the game of Monopoly when I was younger and was waiting for the right moment to play with my kids. During the summer when Ava was eight, she asked if we could play and it turned into quite a lesson.

The game started off pretty well for her and she began buying properties and I thought *she* was going to teach *me* a lesson. She was getting a little confident and spending her money on most rolls without thinking about the future. After about 15 minutes, I caught a break and was able to collect the money being stored in the middle. I then proceeded to buy properties and, eventually, started placing houses and hotels on these properties. At one point, I had about one-third of the board covered with hotels.

Eventually, the law of averages caught up with Ava and she started to land on these properties and had to pay me a large amount in rent. She then discovered that when it rains, it pours, as she could not catch a break and began to land on some of my expensive properties (yes, I had houses on Park Place and Boardwalk).

She ran out of money and told me how unfair this was to her and how lucky I was. Here was my turn to strike. Yes, she did have some bad breaks, and I did have a little luck, but I explained that she also had made unwise decisions in buying everything she landed on without planning for the future, and I had slowly built up my properties over time, not all at once. I explained that in real life, the rich often get richer not because of luck, but because they choose to make the correct decisions (I know there are some people who have struck it rich, but most build it up over time). Rich people get wealthier because they continue to do the same things that made them rich in the first place. The opposite is also true many times—people remain broke because they continue to take the same actions that made them broke in the first place.

After a few more rolls, I started to have a little fun with her. She did not have a dollar to her name nor any property. She landed on one of my hotels again and could not pay. I told her she had to rub my feet. Her look was priceless. I explained that she was now at my mercy—she had no options except to do as I said. She chose to spend her money foolishly and now owed some to me. What other choice did she have but to listen and do whatever I wanted her to? I eventually let her know that I was just kidding about the foot rub but wanted to point out to her what can happen if she is foolish with her money. She learned the lesson—if one continues to make foolish decisions they will eventually have a price to pay, which could be much worse than a foot rub.

The Magic of Compound Interest

Now can also be a great time to teach your child about the magic of compound interest. Here is a neat way to show how it works. Ask your child would he rather have $1,000 right now or a penny that doubles in value every day for one month. I am sure you probably see there is a catch and selected the penny but your child may select the $1,000. To show you how right you are, this penny would be worth over $5 million after 30 days. Here's how:

Day	Amount	Day	Amount
1	$0.01	16	$327.68
2	$0.02	17	$655.36
3	$0.04	18	$1,310.72
4	$0.08	19	$2,621.44
5	$0.16	20	$5,242.88
6	$0.32	21	$10,485.76
7	$0.64	22	$20,971.52
8	$1.28	23	$41,943.04
9	$2.56	24	$83,886.08
10	$5.12	25	$167,772.16
11	$10.24	26	$335,544.32
12	$20.48	27	$671,088.64
13	$40.96	28	$1,342,177.28
14	$81.92	29	$2,684,354.56
15	$163.84	30	$5,368,709.12

This is definitely an extreme example but is meant to show your child how fast something can compound. A way you can make this a real life example for your child is to offer to match dollar for dollar any savings she saves. However, set up a minimum length of time this amount has to remain saved before you match it. This will teach them the value of delayed gratification. In addition, many companies offer their employees 401k investing accounts in which they offer a matching amount up to a certain percentage the employee invests. Showing this to your child at a young age can show her the importance of investing and how to take advantage of free money.

Summary

During this time period of secondary years, your child is becoming more aware that her actions lead to certain outcomes. If she chooses to study and prepare for a test at school, she will see what this leads to when she gets her score back. She is learning that life is not always fair and some of her friends have more than she does and some have less, some are more athletic and some are less, some are better at school and some, no matter how much they study, seem to perform poorly in their academics.

With these observations, your child is also learning that some people have opportunities and obstacles depending on their strengths and weaknesses. Up until 3rd grade, almost all classmates are "friends." Now she is realizing that some have different values and beliefs than she does, and probably won't ever be her BFF (best-friend forever). This can be sad but also eye-opening for your child.

On the opposite end, your child is now wanting more freedom. She may want to ride her bike to a friend's house down the road; she may not want you to always go on field trips with her; she may choose which friends to invite over and hang out with who are not just the children of Mom and Dad's friends; and she will select the sports and clubs *she* is most interested in participating in. This can be scary for parents, but great for our children. They are beginning to make their own choices and are establishing their own identity in a secure environment. As a parent, you can begin to see which values and habits they have selected, what they enjoy and believe in, and the type of adult they are trying to become.

This is a great age range for parents to really begin to reinforce those values and habits they want their children to understand. The ones outlined in this chapter were:

✓ The Sweet Spot – Find This And You Will Never Feel Like You Are Working

✓ Working Outside The Home – Finding Ways To Earn Money Other Than An Allowance

✓ Opening Doors – The Emergency Fund

✓ Time On Electronics – Budgeting

✓ Monopoly Money – The Borrower Is Servant To The Lender (Debt)

✓ The Magic of Compound Interest

If some of the lessons explained in this chapter seem too advanced for your child right now don't fear; just do your best to find relevant examples for her. You can even come up with your own lessons. You can rest assured that any effort you put into teaching these, or other money habits, is time well spent. Whether *you* teach them or not, your child *will* learn them—she can learn sound financial lessons in a healthy way while she is young, or learn them in a destructive way when she is older and the consequences are dire.

CHAPTER 7

Early Adolescence
Ages 12–14

Let The Games Begin

Early adolescence, ages 12 to 14, could be the last time you have a great influence on your child's money habits and values. Once he reaches the high school years, peers can have a much greater impact. Let's make the most of this opportunity!

During these years, your child is changing in so many ways. We can easily see the physical growth and development your child is going through; however, what is harder to detect is the ability he is starting to possess in understanding more complex information. When children reach the teenage years, they tend to want to become more independent in the choices they make. You can start to clearly see the unique individual characteristics your child exhibits and what he values. He is growing up before your eyes! This increase in financial independence and need for freedom in making choices can be a huge challenge for parents. Therefore, this is a crucial time in your child's life when it comes to developing sound financial habits and values. This is when you get to see if the lessons you have been teaching are having an impact, and you can start building on these to make financial wisdom part of his identity, too.

During these years, your child will develop his own identity. He will start to establish his own morals and values and feelings of self-esteem. His peers will begin to play a larger role in this process. He is starting to seek acceptance in certain peer groups, and the desire to fit in can (and probably will) influence his financial decisions. This will show in the clothes he wears and activities he chooses. He may start to use money as a way to explore his independence.

He is also beginning to develop cognitive reasoning. While his decisions are starting to be made by more logical thinking, many are still impulsive. This is why these early adolescent years can be so challenging for parents. While your child is beginning to make independent decisions, he is often unable to fully comprehend how his current actions have future consequences.

The Value Of Work (Money Doesn't Grow On Trees)

If your parents were like mine, I am sure at some point in your childhood you were told money does not grow on trees. We cannot just go to the bank and continuously pull out money—at some point it will run out. Now is a great time to teach your child that the best way to get more money is the same way that has been around for hundreds of years—to earn it!

I know that 12- to 14-year-olds are not legally able to have a traditional job, but there are some jobs they are allowed to do to earn money outside their chores such as babysitting, mowing the grass, and if they are good with academics, tutoring. This is a great opportunity for them to begin to understand the time and effort it takes to earn money and the purchasing power this time and effort creates. This is a lesson that can last a lifetime!

A good way to begin this lesson is to brainstorm with your child ways he can earn money. You can connect how this money can be used to purchase things he wants like a phone or video games. The less you (the parent) pays for these items, the more powerful the lesson is for your son. I know most of us want our kids to have more than we did, but this desire can have a long-lasting negative effect on what he earns, and has, the rest of his life.

Debit Cards (Using Plastic)
WHAT? GIVE MY TEENAGER A CREDIT CARD!?
WHAT ARE YOU THINKING?!

Please notice the type of card I am suggesting in this section. It is a debit card, not a credit card! Many adults do not use credit cards wisely, so there is **NO WAY** I would ever give a teen a credit card. However, pretty soon your child will be using a piece of plastic to pay for things and if you don't allow him the practice, the results could be very bad.

A great way to teach discipline when using plastic is to allow your child to use a debit card attached to his bank account. He can only spend the money he has. Many of us don't fully understand that any time we pay for anything using a credit card, we are essentially buying that item on loan with no interest for 30 days. However, after this time passes, we now owe interest on this amount. Compound this over a few months and it can start to get scary.

If you have been using the advice given in previous chapters, your child will have had a savings account for a while; but now he is making more frequent transactions. This can make balancing the checkbook more inconvenient. This is often what happens with adults. We want convenience so we go from the responsible (yet more time consuming) checkbook to the dangerous (yet easier) credit card. Once we do this, we are playing with fire. Without being aware of how much we actually have in the bank, we easily lose track of our spending and eventually get burned. Debit cards are a great step for adults and an awesome teaching tool for future adults.

Another great reason to allow your child to use a debit card is so you can see how he is spending his money, and can discuss these purchases with him. You can see the wisdom of some of his purchases, and question him about others. This is the reason so many adults get deeply in debt—they never take the time to analyze how they are spending their money. After making unwise choices for a period of time, they are then hit with huge credit card bills. Allowing your child to use a debit card and discussing the purchases with him is a great way to teach healthy money habits when using plastic.

Since you are modeling good behavior, you also need to discuss the dangers of plastic and why it is important to stay within a budget. Give your child expectations and tell him how often you will monitor his spending habits. If he abuses this privilege, it may be taken away. Most importantly, reassure him that you are always there to discuss his purchases and support him.

Once he is prepared, it is go time. Take him to the bank and let him go through the process of obtaining this card.

Then, go to the store and walk him through the process of using it and then balancing his checkbook. Someone is going to be with him and influence how he feels and what he does in that moment. Who better for that than you?

Welcome To The Real World
(Give them Some Freedom with Large Expenses)

We all have a number of special milestones in our lives. We are often excited and scared at the same time when these occur. The first time we make a large purchase is one of these. Milestones are usually very memorable and give us (the parents) an opportunity to reinforce a habit and/or value that will be remembered for a long time. Identify an upcoming expense that you feel your child is ready to handle and let him have the power to pull the trigger. The purchase could be clothes, a remodel of his room, or an activity to add to the family vacation, for instance.

After you have decided what the expenditure will be, walk him through the way to make a big ticket purchase. Show him how to start researching his options. Allow him to discuss his options with you and do not criticize his reasoning. You can probe and direct a little but you do not want him to be embarrassed to share his thoughts with you. Even if he is making an unwise decision, give him the freedom to do so. Remember, the goal here is to teach. Most of us learn more from our mistakes than our successes. You don't want to create an "I told you so" atmosphere because if your child does mess up, you want him to feel comfortable discussing why this mistake happened.

Here are some tips you can share with your child to help guide him when making this (and any future) purchase:

1. Seek out wise and various counsel and advice.
2. Shop around to find the best deal.
3. Before buying the product, sleep on it.
4. Visualize yourself making the purchase.

Don't let this be an isolated event. Every now and then allow your child to make large purchasing decisions and walk him through the process. Remember, practice makes better. This repeated practice will serve two purposes. Not only will he quickly learn and start to choose the right process; he will also develop self-confidence in making wise choices. Believing you can make wise choices with your money is an important attribute for achieving financial health. Giving your child ample opportunities to do this is a great way for him to start establishing this identity early in his life.

Establishing Long-Term Goals
(Saving For Computers, Cars and College)

It may be difficult to teach a middle-school-aged child the importance of saving for a car or college because the light at the end of that tunnel is so far away. However, when we think about it, this line of thinking happens to adults, too. It can be a great challenge for those in their 20s and 30s to invest money for their retirement. "It's so far away" or "I need this right now, not in 30 years" are some ways we convince ourselves that we need to place a greater priority on a current want rather than save for a future event we cannot picture today.

Learning how to listen to, and take advice from, those who are wiser and more knowledgeable is a great habit to possess. When your child gets to that moment in the future and has the money to buy what he has been saving so long for, he will remember your guidance, be thankful for it, and (most likely) be open to accepting more in the years to come.

To get started with this, help your child select a long-term purchase or expense that will be VERY important to him later. This will be something that is not particularly important today, but has the potential to be the most important purchase in his short life someday. After coming up with this, teach/model the process for setting (and saving for) long term goals.

Here is the process that one of my friends uses with his teenagers:

1. Set a goal that is difficult but achievable.
2. Make the goal something very specific.
3. Break up the goal into small increments.
4. Establish minimum expectations.
5. Publicize it – tell others close to you.
6. Get started right away.

You may have a better process to teach this—that is great! The most important thing is not that you have the best process, but that you teach/model a process for your child in a healthy learning environment.

Don't Bail Your Child Out (Teach By Not Saving the Day!)

While the ultimate goal of this book is to help your child learn how to manage money in a responsible manner, he will still blow some of his money on junk when he has the freedom to do so. This is okay. Even as adults with fully-developed brains, WE still mess up. One of the smaller goals is to allow your child to make mistakes in order to learn important habits and values first-hand. He gets to make these mistakes when the dollar amount is still small. A $100 mistake now is much better than a $10,000 one years from now! These mistakes are good—don't be afraid of them. In fact, treasure them because they are golden opportunities to teach.

The key word to remember is to TEACH. Every action you make (both good and bad) is being carefully watched by your child. A big lesson you want to allow him to learn is that if/when he wastes money on minor things, he will not be able to save up for major items. As parents, most of us want our children to never experience any type of pain whatsoever. When your child is on the verge of making a financial mistake, we (the parents) have to go against what our hearts are telling us and let him do it.

Children have to learn priorities, especially when it comes to money. Giving your child the freedom to spend money however he pleases can lead to trouble (which is a good thing in this case). Of course you want to encourage him to make wise decisions; but when things go south (as they sometimes will), let it happen. The consequences for these decisions may be sad and depressing for your child. However, you must let these occur because they are real, and must be felt by him for the lesson to be effective.

As a parent, one of our natural instincts is to protect our child from experiencing any pain. In this case, protection will actually do more harm than good. If your child blows his money, he will not experience physical harm; the harm will just be emotional and/or financial. If you bail him out, you have established a horrible precedent for the future and missed out on a natural and important teaching opportunity.

Please don't be afraid of the mistakes your child makes. In addition, teach him not to fear these mistakes either. He will fail many times in life. These will happen in school, sports and in relationships. When these moments occur, your role is to comfort, console and encourage him. Pick him up, dust off the bruises and send him back out to play the game, stronger than before. This can only happen if you do not bail him out!

Lead By Example (Practice What You Preach)

Teenagers are making new discoveries almost every day and one thing they will realize is that you—the parent—are not perfect (even if you claim to be). They are beginning to notice your mistakes and may even point them out. Even if they do not say anything, you can be assured they are watching and making mental notes.

One of the most important things you can model right now is to practice what you preach. When he was younger your child may not have noticed your mistakes; he pretty much just figured that you did what you taught. Middle-schoolers are not like this. They know how hard it is to follow your advice and they are watching you to see if you are strong enough to put it into practice yourself. If you aren't, they may feel that it is okay if they don't either.

Remember that no one is perfect—do not try and hide your weaknesses. If there is something you want your children to learn, but this is an area of struggle for you, admit it. Discuss why this is a challenge for you and tell them what your mistakes have cost you. Teaching them it is okay to mess up and then forgive yourself is a healthy habit to instill. Make sure that what you expect of them, and what you expect of yourself, is consistent. If you don't, they will notice and this may cause more damage than if you did not teach them this at all.

Summary

The pre- and early-teenage years are a time full of change. These changes are both visible in the form of physical ones and not so visible in the form of emotional ones. Your child is also beginning to view the world around him differently. He is starting to want more independence and is beginning to understand the characteristics that make him unique. Instead of fearing this new-found growth, embrace and look forward to it. Your child is becoming more mature and is able to comprehend lessons with more understanding. He is starting to establish his own identity. Use this opportunity to help guide him towards establishing healthy personal, moral, ethical and financial values.

Since your child is just starting to develop more mature problem-solving skills, he still needs you to provide some guardrails; however, you also need to give him the chance to fail, to feel the consequences of this mistake, and most importantly, learn from it so he doesn't make this same mistake in the future when the stakes are much higher. In addition, don't forget that your child is also watching you and learning from your actions. A healthy you is a powerful teacher. The lessons we discussed in this chapter were:

✓ The Value Of Work – Money Doesn't Grow On Trees

✓ Debit Card – Using Plastic

✓ Welcome To The Real World – Give them Some Freedom with Large Expenses

✓ Establishing Long-Term Goals – Saving For Computers, Cars and College

✓ Don't Bail Your Child Out – Teach By Not Saving the Day!

✓ Lead By Example – Practice What You Preach

This may be the last opportunity you have to greatly influence your child's habits and values with money. Make the most of it!

CHAPTER 8
High School Years
Ages 15–18

Your Child Can See The Light At
The End Of The Tunnel

Your child is now of the age where she can see the light at the end of the tunnel towards adulthood. Yes, she is still a few years away, but life after high school will be here before she (and you) know it. Now is the time to discuss more mature financial issues with her.

You want to start helping her take control of her future. If she doesn't learn how to manage her own money, others will find ways to do it for her. With the recent economic downturn, there have been many stories showing how some in powerful positions have taken advantage of others. From CEOs to mortgage brokers, there are those who will prey upon those who know little about money. Now is a great time to start talking to your child about the role of money. Sit down with her and go over your bills in depth. Show her why she cannot have everything her friends have. I am sure that some of her friends will be driving cars much nicer than she does; heck, these cars may even be fancier than YOUR car. Let her see how much the mortgage and electric bills are. Many families never discuss financial matters—some are even more comfortable talking about sex than finances. Don't miss this valuable opportunity to teach your child about money.

Self-Control

A great topic you can really start getting into during this period is self-control. It is so important that we learn how to delay gratification. Many of us do not set long-term goals and instead spend money on things we truly don't need. I feel this is one of the main reasons that so many got themselves into a financial bind. We live in a time where it is hard to delay gratification. We see something we like and we buy it; often without giving any thought to the future ramifications of these decisions. During these ages, help your teen develop a plan that will give measurable results. For example, have her make a goal of saving $25 each month. This is something that is achievable for most and also easy to keep track of. She could also set aside a certain amount each month to buy a more expensive item, an expensive piece of jewelry or even a car (more on this in a bit). The important thing is that she learns how to avoid the temptation of buying something immediately, and instead, delays her satisfaction.

Wants vs. Needs

A topic you can re-visit is Wants versus Needs. Many teens (as well as adults) think that certain things are absolute needs when, in fact, they are not. The teenage years are a good time to discuss this since many teens feel they have to have something just because someone else does. When asked whether they thought it was okay to borrow money to buy clothes or go on vacation, 11% of high school students surveyed by the Jump$tart Coalition agreed it was okay.

What constitutes a need and/or a want can be relative to our particular situation and time in life (I know some teens who think their phone is the most important thing they have); but from our elementary school days, most of us know that our only needs to survive are food, air, water and shelter. Discussing this topic again when your child is more mature can be a great reminder for her.

There Is A Cure For The Summertime Blues –
The Value of Work

This is also a great time to talk about the value of work. Having a car is a major expense and motivating factor for most teens. My parents taught me a great lesson when I was looking to buy my first car. I began working when I was 14 years old. My family owned an appliance business and I delivered and set up appliances during my summer break. My parents agreed to match the amount I earned and I could apply this towards my car. Instead of hanging out with my friends all summer, I lifted heavy appliances in the hot Florida sun. I continued to do this in the afternoons once school started. By the time I turned 16, I had saved $2,000! With my parents matching this amount, I had enough to buy a $4,000 car. My grandfather was looking to purchase a new vehicle and was kind enough to sell me his truck for the amount I had. This was my first real understanding of money.

I realized if I worked hard and saved, I could buy something that I desired. I was fortunate that my parents gave me money, but even more fortunate that they made me work to earn their matching amount. Some of my friends had their cars and other items bought for them by their parents, and let me tell you, they did not treat their possessions like I did mine. I valued what I had because I knew how much sweat had gone into earning it.

Another reason that work is important is that it can be a great motivator to do well in school. One of my good friends has a teenage daughter who just got her first job. After her first weekend of work, she talked about how tired she was. I thought this was great! Think back to your first job—would you want to still be doing that today? Many of us would say absolutely not! As I just mentioned, my first job was delivering and setting up appliances in hot and humid South Florida. If something like that is your passion I say go for it; for me, it was not. If your child does get a job that is physically draining, it is a great time to explain why getting a good education is so important. Doing well in school is not the end-all be-all but it can open doors that would otherwise remain closed and give your child more options in life.

Flipping Burgers – Looking At Work As An Opportunity

As a teacher, I see first-hand how entitled some of our younger generation feel. Some think they "deserve" certain things. This line of thinking is not going to bode well for them once they enter the real world. In fact, some would even look at certain jobs as being beneath them.

Charles Sykes discusses this in his book *50 Rules Kids*

Won't Learn In School: Real-World Antidotes to Feel-Good Education with the topic of working at a fast-food restaurant. He says, "Flipping burgers is not beneath your dignity. Your grandparents had a different word for burger flipping. They called it opportunity. You live in a country with extraordinary opportunity and income mobility: if you start at the bottom, that doesn't mean you will stay there. The important thing is to actually start."

How true is this? Your child may not want to be a hamburger-flipper, but she can be the best hamburger-flipper ever, and through hard work and applying herself, will soon move up to manage the burger flippers. Once again, using this same initiative, she can become the best manager of these workers and will move up and become manager of the entire store. Continuing to do this, she will move all the way up the ladder over time. It is all in how you to choose to look at the job—some will complain about how unfair it is and not apply themselves, whereas others will look at this as an opportunity to learn and become better at something. The decision is up to the individual.

This reminds me on an episode from the television series *Friends*. In one episode, two of the characters, Monica and Phoebe, are throwing a surprise party for their friend Rachel. For those of you who have never seen *Friends*, Monica is a control freak and naturally takes over planning the party. She puts Phoebe in charge of ice and cups. Pretty boring job, huh? Well, Phoebe takes advantage of this opportunity and is actually the hit of the party. She makes everything imaginable out of cups (cup hat, cup banner, cup chandelier), and serves every kind of ice along with snow cones. Phoebe used the opportunity she was given and turned it into something great.

I know the recession has had an impact on the number of jobs open for teens compared to a few years ago, but there are many possibilities for your child to work. Here are a few areas that might be a good fit for her:

Mow grass
Babysit
Pet-sit
Dog walking
Tutor
Computer lessons/help
Washing/detailing cars
Painting houses
Lifeguard
Summer camp counselor
Waiter/Hostess
Referee/Umpire

If none of these are a fit, your child might have to get creative. For example, Ava told me she wanted to write a book. Since she showed interest in this, I explained to her that writing a book could lead to income if it got published and people bought it. At the very least, I knew she would continue to use her brain over the summer in pursuing this income-generating idea.

Helping Your Child – Preparing For A Job Interview

If your teen is able to secure an interview for a job, she will probably be very nervous. Here are some tips that can help prepare her a little better:

Arrive 10 minutes early for the interview

This is not early enough to look too needy but will show that your teen is eager and excited for the job. If your teen is not sure where to go, have her get directions ahead of time. In fact, have your teen take a test drive to this place before the day of the interview so she can see what to expect from the traffic going there. Your child will most likely be very anxious on interview day—try to eliminate anything that could go wrong so that she can focus on the interview itself and not on other factors.

Dress appropriately

Khakis and a shirt with a collar is great for guys and a skirt and blouse for ladies. The clothes your child wears to the mall and hanging out with friends are probably not a good choice. In addition, any type of piercings besides earrings for girls, are probably not good to showcase during this interview.

Be prepared and don't just show up for the interview

The more information your teen has prepared in advance, the better impression she will make on the interviewer. She should bring the following to the interview:

- Completed job application (if the employer doesn't have it already)
- Working papers
- References
- Resume (if available)
- Note pad
- Pen

Know Your Schedule

Your child should know what days and hours she is available to work—the employer will most likely ask. It probably goes without saying but flexibility is definitely an asset. The more time your teen is available, the easier it is for the employer to set a work schedule. Your teen should also know how she is going to get to and from work—is she doesn't drive, or even if she does and will need to borrow a car.

Go on Your Own

I know this is a hard one for us parents, but if you bring your teen to an interview, don't go into the interview room with her—this is something she needs to do solo. It is important that your child speaks for herself and connects with the interviewer without your assistance.

Make an Impression

It's essential to have good manners when interviewing. Your child should shake the interviewer's hand upon meeting her—firm and not wimpy. She should not sit until she is invited to do so. Your teen should sit straight up in the chair and not slouch. Your teen should also be careful not to use slang or swear. A good way to break the ice is for your child to notice something in the office (a family photo, piece or art, etc.) and ask about it.

After the interview is over, your teen should thank the interviewer for her time and follow this up with a handwritten thank-you card. Most importantly, have your teen focus on being polite, positive, and professional throughout the interview and answer all of the questions to the best of her ability. Remind her it is okay if she does not get this particular job. Any interview will be good practice for what she will most likely do throughout her working life.

Typical Interview Questions

Try to remember your first job interview. Most of us were very nervous and unsure what questions would be asked of us. To help your teen in this area, here are some potential questions she may be asked along with possible answers to these questions.

Question: Why are you looking for a job?
Answer: My parents are matching the amount I earn for my first car so I will be working to save up for that.

Question: Why do you feel you are the best candidate for this job?
Answer: Because I'm responsible, reliable, and a hard worker.

Question: Why are you interested in working for our company?
Answer: I have heard great things about you and want to be a part of your team.

Question: Do you have any experience in this type of work?
Answer: Not exactly, but I am a fast learner and want to learn as much as I can about (blank).

Question: How has school prepared you for working at our company?
Answer: I have had to learn how to budget my time accordingly which will help me be able to focus solely on my job while I am at work.

Question: Have you ever had difficulty with a supervisor or teacher?

Answer: I have disagreed with some of my teachers but have been able to voice my concerns in a calm and respectful way.

Question: What has been your most rewarding accomplishment?
Answer: Last semester, I studied very hard and made straight "A"s.

Question: Tell me about a strength of yours.
Answer: I'm a good listener and I like to be around people.

Question: Tell me about a weakness of yours.
Answer: I've been called a perfectionist, but I like to do things right.

Question: Are you available on weekends?
Answer: Yes I am. And if ever I'm not, I'll be sure to let you know in advance.

Question: Tell me about how you would handle a difficult customer.
Answer: I would politely listen to their complaint without interrupting them and then try to help them solve the problem.

Question: How would you handle working with someone you didn't particularly like?
Answer: I get along easily with people. I don't think that would be a problem.

Question: How would you describe your ability to work as a team member?

Answer: I am a member of my school's football team (or some other team/organization) and I have had to work together with a team to achieve our goals.

Question: What position do you think would fit you best?
Answer: I would like to learn as many different positions and jobs as I can. I'm really flexible.

Question: Do you have your own transportation?
Answer: Yes (if you do) or I don't have my own car, but my parents have agreed to drive me to work.

Question: Why should I hire you?
Answer: Because I have a positive attitude and I'll work hard every day.

Before the actual interview, have your child practice answering these questions. Conduct a mock interview (or a few interviews—practice makes better) with you (the parent) acting as the potential employer. The more comfortable your child is, the more likely she will do well on the job interview.

Keeping Track Of Your Money – Balancing A Checkbook

Many teens get a part-time job once they turn fifteen. If this is the case, now is a great time to talk about those things associated with employment. One such item is balancing a checkbook. Jump$tart Coalition did a survey on financial literacy with high school students. According to this study, only 45% of the high school seniors surveyed had a checking account. Once they go off to college and are more or less on their own, they begin making mistakes. Thirty percent of college students surveyed admitted to bouncing a check. Once your child gets a job and/or begins earning money, take her to a bank to open checking and savings accounts. Teach her how to write a check and balance a checkbook. She can even get a debit card to help her manage her money better. Don't wait until she is on her own when financial mistakes can be more costly.

The Only Sure Things Are Death and Taxes – Uncle Sam

Once your child has a job, it is a great time for her to learn about Uncle Sam. Many adults, let alone teens, know almost nothing about taxes. Once your child earns her first paycheck, sit down with her and explain what is on her pay stub.

For instance, your child might have worked 40 hours and gotten paid $8 an hour, however her check will not be for $320. That will be the gross amount, what she earned before deductions are taken out. Everyone has to have deductions taken from their paychecks which are listed on your paystub. Mandatory deductions include those for Federal and State income taxes, Social Security (FICA) and Medicare. You could also have voluntary deductions taken out. These can include health insurance, dental insurance, disability insurance and retirement savings.

Now is a great time to discuss these deductions with your child since she will feel the pain of not having as much money as she thought she earned. In addition, when it comes time to file a tax return, have her sit down with you (or your accountant) so that she can learn about this, too. This is a natural time to discuss what some of our tax money pays for. Some of the items our taxes help pay for include our military, police, prisons, firefighters, teachers/schools, libraries, roads and public parks. Many people complain about paying taxes (I know I have sometimes when it comes to paying for things I don't agree with) but most of this money is put to good use.

Saving Your Money – Bank Accounts

After your child does earn a paycheck, it is an opportune time for her to open a bank account (if she has not already done so). There are two basic types of bank accounts—checking and savings. A checking account allows you to keep your money in a safe place until you need it to buy something or pay a bill. With the advent of debit cards, these accounts are more useful now since you don't have to write a check to pay for many transactions, you can merely swipe a card. The pitfall of these accounts is that your child has to keep up with her balance. Show her how to balance a checkbook and keep up with this account.

A savings account is a place to store money for the future —not for next Friday night. A plus to these accounts is that they pay interest. This is a great place for your child to start placing money for those down-the-road purchases such as living expenses while she is in college, car insurance and maybe even a future down payment on a house.

Throwing Money Away – Credit Cards

While we are on the topic of bank accounts and debit cards, now is an ideal time to discuss that other card—the credit card. I would never recommend you open a credit card in your child's name to help her establish credit. Such cards can be very dangerous when not used properly.

Explain to your child why credit cards can be so hazardous to her financial future. There is a reason many of us get numerous offers in the mail each week and it is not because we are a valued customer. Once you get behind the eight ball and are in debt it can be a very tough climb out of it. Many young adults accumulate debt buying pizza or their beverage of choice without thinking about the future ramifications of this debt. Even though paying the minimum looks very affordable, you have to plug in the numbers to discover the true cost of debt. If someone charges $3,000 on a credit card with an 18% interest rate and just pays the minimum amount each month, it will take almost 22 years to get rid of this debt!

Saving For The Future – Compound Interest

I know it may seem early, but now is also a great time to talk with your child about saving for the future. Many teens (and adults) lack the ability to see one week into the future so getting her to think about retirement can be difficult. However, now is a great time to teach your child about the magic of compound interest. Here is a comparison which shows why it is so important to start investing early.

John and Jeremy were friends since they were little. As they got older, they both knew they should start thinking about their futures. When John turned 19, he decided to invest $2,000 every year (under $167 a month) for eight years. He picked mutual funds that averaged 12% growth each year. Once he hit 26, John stopped investing. So he put a total of $16,000 into his investment funds. On the flip side, Jeremy waited until he had a better-paying job at age 27 before saving for retirement. Just like John, he put $2,000 into his investment funds every year until he turned 65. He earned the same 12% growth as John but invested 31 more years than John did. He ended up investing a total of $78,000 over 39 years. Fast forward to when they both turned 65. Who do you think had more? John, with his total of $16,000 invested over eight years, or Jeremy, who invested $78,000 over 39 years? It turns out John came out way ahead! Jeremy had a total of $1,532,166, while John had a total of $2,288,996. How is this possible? Well, John had the power of compound interest on his side longer than Jeremy and, thus, came out over $700,000 ahead of Jeremy even though he invested a lot less.

Here's an easy way to teach your kids about compound interest. Let's say you invest $100 and this investment averages a 9% return a year. Because of compound interest this money will double in eight years. The chart below shows you how this works.

Year	Money Earned from Interest	Total Amount of Money
0	$0.00	$100.00
1	$9.00 (9% of $100.00)	$109.00
2	$9.81 (9% of $109.00)	$118.81
3	$10.69 (9% of $118.81)	$129.50
4	$11.66 (9% of $129.50)	$141.16
5	$12.70 (9% of $141.16)	$153.86
6	$13.85 (9% of $153.86)	$167.71
7	$15.09 (9% of $167.71)	$182.80
8	$16.45 (9% of $182.80)	$199.26

I know it is difficult for most teens (along with many adults) to see past the next weekend, but if your teen can set a relatively small amount of her income aside to invest, it can pay off big time in the long run. Let's say your 16-year-old finds a way to invest only $25/month once she begins working. That is around what it would cost to go to the movies one time when you factor in the price of a movie ticket, soda and popcorn so this is not too big of a sacrifice. If she continued to invest just this $25 each month until she turned 65 and earned a modest 8% a year on this, she will have over $182,000! With this amount she could build her very own theater room in her house.

Now your child can see how a small amount of money can turn into a lot. Even Albert Einstein had an opinion concerning compound interest. Rumor has it he said the following, "Compound interest is the eighth wonder of the world. He who understands it, earns it. . . he who doesn't. . . pays it." It is pretty difficult to disagree with the man often referred to as the father of modern physics.

Debt Free University – Paying For College

Since many college students have to take out some sort of student loan to pay for at least some of their schooling now is an ideal time to discuss how your daughter will finance college. Many young adults don't think twice about racking up large student debts. Like I mentioned before, I know for some people, getting a student loan is the only way they'll be able to attend college; so it can be a good investment for many. But I would advise you to sit down with your teen and explain how these loans work. Many college students do not work, so they borrow enough to pay for their living expenses as well as tuition and other student fees. I encourage you to explain to her that she will have to start paying towards this loan once she graduates, when she is just starting out in life and will have many other expenses to worry about. If your child does need to obtain a student loan, my advice is that she uses it for educational expenses only and gets a job to pay for her living expenses.

According to Mark Kantrowitz, publisher of FinAid.org and FastWeb.com, the average student loan debt for new graduates has reached **$27,300**. Add to that the loans some parents took out to help pay for their child's education and that number goes up to **$34,400**. Some experts even say that student loan debt is more toxic than mortgages because this debt cannot be forgiven—even if you file for bankruptcy.

In fact, student loan debt is now something that could have severe consequences for our economy. Two-thirds of the class of 2011 held student loans upon graduation, and the average borrower owed $26,600, according to a report from the Project on Student Debt by the Institute for College Access and Success. That's up 5% from 2010 and is the highest level of debt in the seven years the report has been published. In addition, as students accumulate more debt, they are also having a harder time repaying it. According to the U.S. Department of Education, the percentage of borrowers who defaulted on their federal student loans within two years of their first payment jumped from 8.8% to 9.1% in fiscal year 2011.

It is estimated that the grand total of all student loan debt exceeds $1 trillion—this amount is greater than total household consumer debt! This comes at a time when the job market is not as strong as years past which can have dire consequences for society as a whole. In fact, according to the Pew Research Center, 37% of 18- to 29-year-olds are either under-employed or unemployed. Student loan debt could force many younger adults to delay important milestones many of us reach such as getting married, buying a house and having children. This leads to a slowdown in the housing market which can affect many of us.

Getting a college degree is very important—more on that in a little bit. Despite this, your child has to be smart about college debt or she will find herself in the same spot many are in today. There are some options on limiting the amount you will spend on college. One such option is to attend a community college for two years before transferring to a larger four-year college. I know some careers value where a degree is earned but many (including teaching) do not take this into account when it comes to hiring and determining pay. In fact, as a teacher, I would get paid the same amount whether I graduated from Harvard or The University of Georgia. Community College can be a great way for some to begin their college careers.

Student loans make sense if you have not saved enough money for your child to attend college, if your child needs one in order to attend college (she did not receive a scholarship or enough financial aid) or if your child cannot work enough to pay for school because her grades would suffer.

There are two basic types of student loans—federal (government) loans and private loans. Federal student loans are ideal because they usually have a low interest rate and are available to students who may not have much of a credit history. There are two types of federal student loans—The Stafford Loan or the Perkins Loan.

Stafford Loan

Stafford Loans are made available to college and university students to supplement personal and family resources, scholarships, grants and work-study. Nearly all students are eligible to receive Stafford Loans regardless of credit. Stafford Loans may be subsidized by the U.S. Government (for students with financial need) or unsubsidized (no financial need required) depending on the student's need.

A Stafford Loan has many benefits. They have a low fixed interest rate—at the writing of this book it was 3.86% with borrowing limits up to $31,000 per year depending on degree status and years in school. Students do not have to pay for these while enrolled in school, and acceptance for this type of loan is not based on credit. In addition, there is a six-month grace period (the six months after the student leaves college) before the student has to start paying on this debt.

Perkins Loan

The Perkins Loan Program provides low interest loans to help needy students finance the costs of postsecondary education. Students attending one of the participating postsecondary institutions can obtain Perkins Loans from the school.

Each school's revolving Perkins Loan fund is replenished by ongoing activities, such as collections by the school on outstanding Perkins Loans made by the school and reimbursements from the Department for the cost of certain statutory loan cancellation provisions.

Students must file a *Free Application for Federal Student Aid (FAFSA)* as part of the application process for a Perkins Loan. Students also will need to complete a Perkins promissory note in order to receive a loan.

One very beneficial aspect of a Perkins Loan is that borrowers are eligible for loan cancellation for teacher service at low-income schools and under certain other circumstances. Also, students may defer repayment of the loan while enrolled (at least half-time) at a postsecondary school. A borrower who has difficulty repaying a Perkins Loan can contact the school where she received the loan to find out if she is eligible for a deferment or forbearance based on economic hardship or other circumstances.

The Party's Over – Life After School

Once your child is in high school, I feel it is extremely important to start the conversation about what her life will look like when she becomes an adult. I know I am biased (being a school teacher) but most recent unemployment statistics show why having an education is so important; probably more now than ever before. According to the Bureau of Labor Statistics, in 2011 the unemployment rate for those without a high school diploma was 50% higher than those with a high school diploma and almost three times higher than those with a college degree.

I know that having a college degree does not guarantee success nor is it the end-all be-all. You still have to work hard and be productive. However, a degree does open doors that would otherwise remain closed. I was recently reminded of this a couple of summers ago when I decided to paint the outside of our house. I got a quote for someone to do this and it was $3,000. I could buy all the materials and do the labor myself (the hard part) and save my family over $2,500. Now, the middle of June was not very pleasant here in Georgia. We had many 90-degree-plus days during my painting time. I came in after painting for eight hours completely drenched with sweat. I pointed this out to my daughters and told them why it is so important to get a college degree since this will give them options they might not otherwise have—if I did not have a degree, my job might have been a painter instead of a teacher. I have to admit it was not as bad as I thought, but painting a house is not something I am passionate about. I know some people would love this job and I say more power to them. For me, I am glad I have a degree so that I have many opportunities.

I still remember when I realized how important getting a college degree would be. As I mentioned earlier, my family owned an appliance business while I was growing up in Florida. I started working for them delivering and setting up appliances when I was 15. I continued to do this most summers and into my early college days. My first year of college was not my best academically speaking. I fooled around too much and did not focus at all on my school. This was reflected in my grades. That summer I went back to work delivering appliances to earn some spending money. My family's company got a job to install washers and dryers in a retirement community. There were at least 20 buildings in this community and I had to install two sets of washers and dryers in each building— one downstairs and the other upstairs. Let me tell you, summer in Florida is not very pleasant if you are outside doing manual labor. Some mornings it can feel like 100 degrees (with the humidity) by 9 a.m.

One day I started to analyze my situation. I realized that if I kept messing around in college I might not get a degree and would have to deliver appliances for the rest of my life. I was okay doing this when I was 19, but knew I did not want to do this the rest of my life. I decided then and there that I was going to apply myself and do better in school.

The very next semester I earned straight "A"s and made the President's List. I know many successful people did not graduate from college, and a degree does not automatically guarantee success, but the numbers do not lie—a college degree will help keep you employed, even in difficult economic times.

Yes, A Teacher Is Writing This – Why College Is Not Always A Good Option

I just made the argument why it is so important to obtain a college degree and now am going to play devil's advocate. As a school teacher I value a quality education. However, I am starting to question how important a college degree is.

When I think of what we (educators) teach, a lot of it involves staying within a certain structure. This is the reason that a lot of entrepreneurs did not have success in college and dropped out before getting a degree—people such as Mark Zuckerberg, Bill Gates and Steve Jobs. Now I know these three are definitely not the norm, but they do show that even if one decides to start a business instead of earning a B.A. she can still be successful.

As a parent, of course I want my daughters to attend college. But I do wonder if this is embedded in us because this was the "right" thing to do for so many years. In this day and age, one can be very successful running an online business (or something else) that does not require four years and a lot of money to start. What do you feel is the better choice—starting a business that you are passionate about with a small upfront fee that takes a while to build but grows each year, or going to school for four years (or more) and graduating with a large amount of student loan debt that will take ten years to pay off? Sometimes I feel we push our children into earning a degree that will ultimately do them more harm than good.

I recently watched an interview with the rapper and entrepreneur 50 Cent. I know a lot of us (including myself) have an image of rappers and most of these do not fit Fiddy. After this interview, I remember talking with Tracy about how impressed I was with him and that his knowledge did not come from books or four years of studying various topics; it came from pursuing his passions and adapting and growing along the way—things that cannot be learned by sitting in a room listening to a lecture. I don't mean to discourage you from wanting your child to attend college, but do hope that maybe I can give you a different perspective. If your daughter decides to start her own business or pursue a passion instead of attending college, this may actually be a very wise decision. Instead of spending a huge amount of money to "discover herself" and taking four years to figure this out, she will get an immediate lesson of what it takes to be successful in the kind of life she is hoping to live.

Take A Year Off From School – A Gap Year

To start with, a "gap year" usually describes a year off between high school and college. They have been a common practice in England and other countries for some time and have recently gained popularity in the United States. In fact, according to the Higher Education Research Institute at UCLA, around 1.2% of first-time college freshmen choose to defer enrollment for a year. Gap years offer an opportunity to travel, explore different interests, and gain experience and maturity before beginning college.

Many students choose to take a gap year because they see it as an opportunity to try something new and take a break from schooling; at the same time, they can gain a new perspective that will benefit them in their college careers and beyond.

A gap year can be a great opportunity to pursue an interest or passion and gain experience that will be attractive to employers after graduation.

Holly Bull, president of The Center for Interim Programs, a company that offers parents and students consulting in choosing the appropriate gap year program says, "In 1980, no one was talking gap year. I've watched this whole concept go basically from its inception to present day. I wouldn't call it mainstream, but there's way more awareness and support and colleges are now beginning to endorse it as a really positive thing." With over 20 years of experience researching gap years, Bull has seen students work everywhere from outdoor education centers to Scottish castles to elephant sanctuaries. She says the students who come to her are often looking for a break from the academic grind.

The gap year can provide young people an opportunity to learn what type of adult they want to be. It can also help them gain more focus so that they don't have to spend extra years, and tuition dollars. "I'm definitely hearing from families that it's harder to consider these colleges' tuitions with a student who seems so uncertain," Bull says. With the rising costs of education, this may be an option for your child to gain a skill that will benefit her for a lifetime.

Do Whatever You Want – Freedom

Now may also be a great time to discuss how much freedom your child has. Many of us have the most freedom we will ever have when we are high school seniors. Many do not have children, mortgages, student loan debt and those other things that come along with life as we get older. If your child wants to travel to Spain and sell artwork after she graduates, now is probably the best opportunity she will ever have. I know you might think this may not be the most responsible thing to do at this point in time but it is true. Once we start getting older, we have many more responsibilities that make it much harder to drop everything and do something like this. If your child wants to backpack through Italy for a few months it might be hard for you to be happy about this, but she may learn more from this experience than what any type of school could teach.

Summary

This can be the most challenging age group to teach. Many teens 15–18 can act so mature one minute and like a 5-year-old the next. However, now is the time when they can see the light at the end of the tunnel, and thus, are better able to relate the skills you teach them to their own lives.

For instance, having a job can often be a huge wake-up call—I know it was for me. Your child can now understand you at a level that she could not before. Having to wake early and forgo something enjoyable to go to work is often a lesson only learned through doing. You can talk about how tough your job is or how bad a day at the office you had, but until your child has a similar experience it is hard for her to relate.

Although this can be a sometimes tough phase for you to relate to, it can also be extremely rewarding. Your little girl is becoming a young woman before your eyes. With this maturity comes greater responsibility and more in-depth lessons and skills needed. Some of the skills we covered in this chapter include:

✓ Self-Control

✓ Wants vs. Needs

✓ The Value of Work – There Is A Cure For The Summertime Blues

✓ Looking At Work As An Opportunity – Flipping Burgers

✓ Potential Jobs For Teens – Work = The Best Place To Go For Money

✓ Preparing For A Job Interview – Helping Your Child

✓ Balancing A Checkbook – Keeping Track Of Your Money

✓ Uncle Sam – The Only Sure Things Are Death and Taxes

✓ Bank Accounts – Saving Your Money

✓ Credit Cards – Throwing Money Away

✓ Saving For The Future – Compound Interest

✓ Paying For College – Debt Free University

✓ Life After School – The Party's Over

✓ Why College Is Not Always A Good Option – Yes, A Teacher Is Writing This

✓ The Gap Year

✓ Freedom – Do Whatever You Want

Congratulations—depending on how old your child is, your job is almost done. Hopefully your child has the financial knowledge and skills to help her do well in the world— especially for those who are ill-equipped. If you find that your child is still lacking, it is not too late to teach her the financial skills she needs to possess before graduating from high school. The best time to plant an oak tree was 30 years ago, the next best time is today! Get busy planting that seed now.

CHAPTER 9
Grown Up
Ages 19 and Up

Yikes! – My Baby Is All Grown Up

Okay, we are now in the home stretch. There are many lessons that your child has hopefully grasped, but the money lessons you can teach during the college years are probably some of the most important pieces of advice you can give him as he prepares to head off into the big (and sometimes scary) world of ours.

Finding Your Purpose

An important thing to discuss is helping your child find his purpose. Most of us were born with certain talents and abilities. Now is a great time to talk about potential career choices with your child to help him choose a path that best suits him. I feel like I was given a gift to teach, both in school and in giving financial advice to others. Even though teaching doesn't pay a large salary, I am content in my profession. In addition, the skills I have developed by teaching children have enabled me to teach adults, too. Talk with your child about finding purpose in life. Encourage him to pursue a career which is rewarding and not just one that pays a large salary.

Does Money Guarantee Happiness?

When discussing your child's gifts and talents, I think it is also a good time to talk about whether money automatically leads to happiness and a satisfying life.

No matter what career path your child selects nor how much he makes, if he spends more than he earns he will eventually be in trouble. It doesn't matter if his salary is $10,000, $100,000, or even $1,000,000 a year; the same principle applies.

There are so many people right now who spend money they don't have—I'm sure you and your child could come up with examples of people you both know who fit into this category. Why do these folks buy things they know they cannot afford? I feel many do it because they are emotionally insecure. We live in one of the wealthiest nations on Earth, yet so many people are unhappy. A great number of Americans seek professional help for this very reason. Clearly, having money can take away many worries, but it doesn't automatically guarantee happiness. Think about some of your peers. Do any of them make a lot of money but have nothing to show for it? There might be some who press the snooze button numerous times on Monday morning because they dread going to work. Even if you make $500,000 a year, if you are unhappy Monday through Friday I don't feel you are "wealthy." Many of these same people spend money and buy things to make themselves "happy." Once the weekend rolls around, they can come up with some great reasons to buy things. "I work so hard and put up with so much that I deserve_____." Fill in this blank with clothes, jewelry, eating out and so on. So many people do this in search of happiness.

Let's face it, buying things can bring about a sense of joy—but only for a moment. If I go out and buy a shirt it feels great. The first few times I wear it, it feels good. Then, after five or six times of wearing this shirt, something happens—it becomes old. How many of us have looked in our closet and said, "I have nothing to wear" even though we have 50 outfits staring back at us? At one point in time we liked these clothes (or at least we liked them enough to buy them) but, after a while, that feeling goes away.

If we base our feelings of happiness on materialistic things, we will be in a constant cycle of having to buy things to make ourselves feel happy. I feel that money problems are 80% emotional. Many people know not to buy things with credit cards that they cannot afford but they still do it. Let's say we use a credit card with a 24% annual percentage rate (APR) and buy something that costs $100. Then we don't make a single payment on this bill the entire year. How much would we owe? If you said $124, you're right: we would pay 2% interest every month (APR/12) = $2/month which totals $24; $100 + $24 = $124. The math is pretty easy but many folks still buy things they don't have the money for. This is where the emotions come into play.

A lot of people are unhappy in their lives—be it spiritually, in their careers, with their spouse, and so on. To combat this unhappiness they buy things. I think that money and weight problems often go hand in hand. We now have easy access to pretty much all of the nutritional information of the food we eat, yet nearly two-thirds of our country is overweight or even obese. We know how bad it is to continually stop by our favorite fast-food restaurant to order a meal and super-size it, but many still do. Why do we do this to ourselves? I feel the answer is the same as why we buy things we can't afford— it gives us a temporary feeling of satisfaction. I know this doesn't apply to everyone but I feel this is a main reason that our nation has become so overweight and in debt. It's simple to have money and be skinny *on paper*. If you lived by the phrase "Eat Less Than You Burn, Spend Less Than You Earn" you would most likely be thin and have money. It sounds so simple, but it can get complicated when emotions get involved.

A Study About Happiness

According to a 2009 study focusing on 450,000 Americans and how they evaluate their happiness, a yearly salary of $75,000 was the number after which people's day-to-day happiness no longer improves. This study was conducted by psychologist Daniel Kahneman and economist Angus Deaton. This tells us that as people earn more money, their day-to-day happiness rises until they hit $75,000. After that it's just more stuff, with no gain in happiness.

This doesn't mean the wealthy and ultra-wealthy are equally happy. Having more money does boost people's life assessment all the way up the income ladder. People who earned $180,000 a year reported more overall satisfaction than people earning $100,000. But, according to Kahneman and Deaton's study, someone making $375,000 a year will not be happier on a day-to-day basis than someone with an annual salary of $75,000, though they will probably feel they have a better overall life.

After reading this study I was intrigued. I knew that teaching ranked among the most satisfying jobs and I wanted to see what other careers ranked high in overall contentment and what their average salaries were. Here is a list of the top 10 most satisfying careers along with their average annual salary:

10	Operating Engineer	$67,200
9	Financial Advisor/Planner	$62,385
8	Psychologist	$78,967
7	Artist	$51,378
6	Education Administrator	$66,061
5	Teacher	$41,193
4	Author	$51,907
3	Physical Therapist	$66,628
2	Firefighter	$44,504
1	Clergyman	$53,200

I must say that unless you write a story about 50 shades of a certain color the author's salary might be high; but all joking aside, I find this list to be very interesting. Only one of these careers averages above that magical $75,000 annual figure, yet many people in these professions are very satisfied and content in their chosen paths. Why is this so? Many of these careers are a calling. The people who have jobs in these fields usually got into them because they are passionate about what they do, first and foremost. These days it's hard to complain about low pay since so many are struggling right now and would love a bigger paycheck; but I think most would agree that a firefighter has to have a passion for rescuing others, willingly risking his life and isn't doing this just for the $44,000 a year he makes. When you have a job that you feel is your calling, you don't need to make a large salary to feel content with it. What a powerful lesson for your child to learn before he enters the working world.

Post-College Job Search

Now that your child hopefully has an idea of what type of career he wants, it is time for the job search. Although the market for recent college graduates has taken a beating during The Great Recession, there is some positive news. According to a 2012 survey by a generation Y research firm, out of 225 employers almost nine in ten say they will hire more graduates this year than last. However, this survey by Millennial Branding, does come with some bad news. Employers report they have been disappointed with the lack of preparation among potential hires during job interviews. Here are some tips for your child to best prepare.

Key Credentials That Impress Employers

Leadership Position—Big Or Small

Around 50% of employers surveyed said they look to hire interviewees who have held leadership positions in on-campus organizations. This could be something as big as student body president or as small as president of the drama club—either one demonstrates the ability to get along with, and work well with, others.

An Internship, Or Two

Your child will not look forward to being an intern since it requires lots of hard work (often for no pay), but many employers say it's the key to landing a job after graduation. In fact, 90% of employers said they look for students who have *at least* one three-month-long internship on their resume (and two is even better), to provide enough experience. This may not sound ideal, but inspiring your child to put in three to six months of work could lead to a lifetime of success.

Research (Yes, More Homework)

Try not to let your child go into a job interview without researching the company—reviewing their website, reading press releases, studying bios and photos. He should also have a thorough understanding of the position he is interviewing for. This may sound like common sense, but many people don't do their homework before an interview. In fact, 40% of employers complained "how unprepared students are in interviews." I am not saying one has to know every little thing about a company, but doing a little research can go a long ways in getting hired.

Ability To Communicate In Real Life

To be successful in any profession requires good communication. According to Dan Schawbel, founder of Millennial Branding, this means "the ability to write, compose emails, give presentations in front of others, and being able to have conversations with those across generations." In this time of constant connection to technology, it is surprising that many young adults lack proper communication skills, but they do. Practicing conversations with family and friends, neighbors—young and old—will help build this important skill. Being able to verbally communicate in a clear, effective manner will help your child stand out from the crowd, and thus, land a job.

A Positive, Upbeat, I-Want-This Attitude

Although this seems like a no-brainer, one in four employers surveyed said they are turned off by candidates' "bad attitudes." This relates back to communication skills. Remind your child that if he doesn't seem excited and eager about working for a company, then why should the boss want to hire him? Even if it is not the job of his dreams, having a positive attitude can go a long way. Encourage your child that no matter what, he should be positive and put his best foot forward; maybe the person he is interviewing with knows someone else who is hiring. Having a great attitude can open many doors that would otherwise stay closed.

Self-Motivated Entrepreneur

One in three employers said they are looking for entrepreneurial experience in their potential hires. Although it might be easier for some teens and college students to work in a more traditional job (delivering pizzas, working at a department store, etc.), starting your own business—even a small online store—can help a student learn more about being an entrepreneur than any class, and at the same time, make them more of a catch to a potential employer.

Look Impressive Online And Always

Any potential employer will probably Google your child's name to see what comes up. In fact, one in three employers said they use social networks to conduct background checks on job candidates, and 40% of those who do said they specifically check Facebook. Now is a great time to check your child's online presence and see if anything needs editing, and instill in him the wisdom that everything he posts can be made public (no matter the privacy setting!) and to never, ever post any words, photos or images that will be detrimental to his future. Remaining respectful in every way is the key— these days children need to be aware that their every word, action or image could be broadcast for the world to see.

Some parents don't want to think about their child getting married and moving away but now is an ideal time to talk about choosing a partner wisely. Remind your soon-to-be adult that, while dating, it's very easy to fall in love and not recognize potential differences in philosophies or life attitudes held by the partner. Tell him to get to really know his soul mate and find out about shared ethical and moral values. Point out to him that this is also the time to discuss with his mate the views they each hold regarding finances. Opposites do attract and in a typical relationship, one partner is usually the saver and the other a spender—this is okay as long as the two see eye to eye on the major financial issues.

In our marriage, Tracy was more of the spender and I was the saver. Over time, we've helped each other see things from the other person's point of view. Tracy is actually tighter with money than I am now, and I have become a little less frugal. A few years ago, Tracy made a skeleton costume for Ava. She used white felt for the bones and glued these onto an inexpensive $5 t-shirt. Shortly after Ava came home from trick-or-treating, I walked into our living room and saw Tracy trying to peel these bones off the t-shirt. I asked why she was doing this and she said it was a perfectly fine t-shirt and was trying to save it. I laughed and said, "We can afford to buy a new t-shirt." Tracy replied, "Why buy another shirt and spend money when I can make this one as good as new?"

Speaking of marriage, you should also begin to talk about your child's wedding day—especially if you have a daughter (or, like me, more than one). Prince William and Princess Kate had what was called The Royal Wedding. Even though I am not a huge fan of weddings and the money they cost, I must admit that I did tune in briefly to watch Kate and William exchange vows. While watching, I looked over at my then 3-year-old daughter (Ella) whose eyes were GLUED to the television set. She was almost in a trance and was mesmerized by Kate's dress. Ella has always been my princess daughter from the time she was old enough to dress herself. She was changing her outfits so much that Tracy and I had to come up with a rule which allowed her to pick out two outfits that she could change into per day. It was getting to the point that she was putting on 10 different dresses a day that we had to hang back up in her closet. I would ask why she kept changing and Ella would respond, "This dress is not pretty." UGH!

I think it is sweet when she dresses up as Cinderella or Snow White but wonder why she is so attracted to princesses. In 2011, my family was interviewed by Christine Romans on CNN's *Your Bottom Line*. Christine asked Ava what she wanted to be when she got older. Ava responded "an artist." This did not surprise me since Ava loves to draw and create. Christine asked Ella this same question and got a much different response. Without any hesitation, Ella answered "a princess." I feel sorry for her future husband!

I wonder why so many girls dream of becoming a princess. I know Disney movies might play a role in this but even as girls grow older and realize these movies are fantasy, they still dream about this. From Ella's point of view, I don't know if it has to do with her watching how much Tracy does at home. I know Tracy and I both feel blessed that she was able to be a stay-at-home mom for nine years, but she still worked extremely hard during this time. Maybe this had an impact on Ella. She saw how much effort Tracy put into making our household run smoothly and all the work it took. I don't know if this has any effect on her, but maybe in her subconscious, she just wants her Prince Charming to come along and take her to his castle. Don't get me wrong, I think the Royal Wedding was very magical. The hard part is it is not a reality. Many people can achieve great success and have rich lives; but it will not likely come in the form of being whisked away to live happily ever after.

Speaking of weddings, many men think about proposing on Valentine's Day thanks to various commercials showing us how magical that is. These ads show how happy our future brides will be, and the couple will live happily ever after. What these commercials don't show is this same couple 10 years down the road when the realities of life (kids, bills and jobs) kick in and that special ring isn't so magical anymore.

The 2008 Wedding Report showed that the average couple spends $3,215 on an engagement ring and another $2,036 on wedding bands. Add that to the $24,066 average wedding (according to www.costofwedding.com) and that adds up to over $29,000 spent on a typical wedding. This money is spent when we least need it—for most, the years you spend dating and the beginning days of being a married couple are usually some of the happiest. Most of us are so in love at this point that we don't need anything else. You might remember those days yourself, when you didn't have much but love and were as happy as could be. Tracy and I actually moved to Poland a few months after getting married. We had no television and even did our laundry in the bathtub for the first month we were there, but were very happy.

I know many little girls dream about their big wedding day, but wouldn't this money be better spent five years later when the babies start coming and money becomes tighter? The $5,000 spent on rings could equal 100 nights of paying a babysitter. The average $24,000 wedding could cover a cleaning lady for 10 years or 240 dinners out at $100 a pop. I am not saying that weddings are not important, but they definitely do not guarantee a happy marriage. Too many people place importance on the size of an engagement ring or the type of wedding dress they are able to wear. These might be important for one day of your life, but they do not help one bit when the kids are keeping you up at night and you desperately need a night out but can't afford it.

I know I may sound unromantic but I feel that I have the best marriage one could ever dream of. Tracy does not have an expensive engagement ring, and although we did have a wedding, it did not cost us nearly as much as the average wedding. Despite that, we are still deeply in love with each other 15 years later. I feel that a lifetime of happiness is worth much more than going into debt for one magical day.

Emergency Fund

In order to have a sound financial plan in place, it is very important to have an emergency fund. Teach your child to be prepared for the unexpected. When talking with your son about money, be sure to discuss the importance of having an emergency fund. He needs to realize that the unexpected does happen—he may lose a job or need a major repair done on his car.

Explain that an emergency fund is completely different from a retirement fund. One should try to never use his retirement accounts to pay for emergencies. Let's say that Jim decides to invest instead of setting up an emergency fund. One day he needs a new air conditioning unit that costs $10,000. He uses some of the money in his 401(k) to pay for this. If Jim is in the 25% income tax bracket, using $10,000 from this account will cost him $2,500 in taxes plus another $1,000 in a penalty for using this money too early. This $10,000 is now worth $6,500 because Jim did not prepare. Help your child avoid making this kind of mistake.

Health Insurance

Many young people feel invincible. Most are in good health and do not feel that anything bad can happen to them; but an uninsured accident or emergency surgery could crush their finances for years. President Obama's health care law lets your child stay on your health insurance plan until he is 26, even if he doesn't live with you and is not your financial dependent, as long as he is not eligible for a policy at his job. If your plan is not an option, your child can look for alternatives at eHealthInsurance (www.ehealthinsurance.com) and the federal government's health resource website (www.healthcare.gov). At the very least your child needs to obtain a catastrophic plan so that he is covered if he has a serious accident or illness.

Credit Card Debt

One of the most important issues you should discuss right now is debt. Many young adults accumulate debt on credit cards without thinking about the future ramifications of this debt. Even though paying the minimum looks very affordable, plug in the numbers and discover the true cost of credit card debt. As I said earlier, if someone charges $3,000 on a credit card with an 18% interest rate and only pays the minimum amount each month, it will take almost 22 years to pay off this debt.

Many young adults will wonder how a credit card company can make money off them if they always make their payment on time. It is great that they have every intention to make that monthly payment on time; but as we wise old adults know, sometimes life gets in the way. In addition, even if one pays the minimum monthly payment each month, he is still paying interest on this balance. The only way to avoid this is to pay off your balance in full each month, or not use a credit card to begin with.

Many people think they are doing well if they just make the minimum monthly payment on their credit cards. Just what is this minimum payment? This is the amount of money you have to pay each month in order to avoid extra fees added on to your balance. In order to remain current with your credit card company, this minimum amount is the least amount they expect you to pay them each month. This minimum payment is based on how much balance you have on the card. The higher the balance, the higher the minimum payment.

To illustrate why even paying the minimum can hurt you in the long run, let's say you have a relatively low credit card balance of $500 with an 18% interest rate. We will say your credit card company sets your minimum monthly payment at $20. Not too bad, you might think. If you divide this $500 by $20 (the monthly payment), you should have this debt paid off in 25 months ($20 x 25 = $500). While that may sound right, you will actually not pay it off in full until paying this amount for 43 months, not 25. How can this be so? Earlier we discussed the magic of compound interest when you had it working for you. This is the complete opposite of that— interest working against you. If you make this $20 payment for 43 months, when all is said and done, you will have paid

$860 ($20 x 43) for this $500 purchase. This is why it is so important to discuss credit cards with your child right now!

Let's say your child wants to know what will happen if he just decides not to pay this debt. First, his creditor will most likely contact him if the payment does not arrive by the due date. They may or may not (depending on past payments) charge a late fee. If your child ignores this request, his account will become delinquent. This means it is official—he is behind in paying this bill. At this point, the credit card company might raise his interest rate, and thus, add a little salt to the wound. If he continues to not pay attention, the next step should make him notice.

At this point, he may start to receive letters in the mail to make him feel nervous about his situation. He may also begin to receive phone calls at the most inconvenient times from collection agents asking for this money. If this doesn't make him take notice, he may get sued by the lender, or if he bought an item with this credit, it could be repossessed. If he continues to keep his head buried in the sand, his creditor might place his account in the charge-off category and not expect to see a dime from him; however, he is still not in the clear. His creditor will probably sell this debt to another company for pennies on the dollar amount he owes. This "new" collection agency will begin calling him, asking if he can just pay something on this debt and hope they can get anything from him (they made a very small investment on collecting this so even if they get him to pay 10% of the balance they will more than likely have made out well). There is really no escaping this. What seemed like a harmless purchase could haunt him well into adulthood.

While discussing debt, it is important to point out that there is some debt that is considered to be "good" debt. Think about the first time you ever borrowed money. What did you borrow this for? Maybe it was to buy something from the school store or a favorite toy. Many times the reason we borrow money is to buy something we do not have the money for at that particular point in time. The thing is, when you borrow money, it ends up costing you in the long run with the interest added to this amount. Although I don't feel that any debt is necessarily good debt, some debt is worth it because it allows you to make a purchase that will pay off more than the original loan in the long term.

An example of this type of debt is a mortgage. Most of us (especially young adults) do not have enough money sitting around to buy a house outright—this is where a mortgage comes into play. Over time, a house should appreciate in value, and unless we want to be homeless, we need a place to live. Another example of good debt is a student loan. Earlier we discussed why it is important to have a college degree. Not everyone is fortunate enough to have all of their college paid for. This is why a student loan is considered good debt—it is debt that will ultimately pay for itself and help you make money in the future. Another example of good debt is money used for purchasing or starting a business. If this business provides a worthwhile product and is managed well, the company should do well, and thus, be a good investment.

To illustrate how ill-prepared some young adults are in handling credit cards, Sallie Mae conducted a report "How Undergraduate Students Use Credit Cards: Sallie Mae's National Study of Usage Rates and Trends, 2009." This report shows that nearly one-third of college students put tuition on their credit card in 2008. In addition, 92% of undergraduate credit cardholders charged textbooks, school supplies or other direct education expenses. Students who used credit cards to pay for direct education expenses estimated charging $2,200. Eighty-four percent of undergraduates had at least one credit card. On average, students have 4.6 credit cards, and half of college students had four or more cards. The average balance of this debt was $3,173. The higher the grade level, the more heavily students used their credit cards, with seniors graduating with an average credit card debt of more than $4,100. The study found that freshmen carried a median debt of $939 and only 15% of freshmen had a zero credit card balance. Many college students seem to use credit cards to live beyond their means—not just for convenience—and more than three-quarters incurred finance charges by carrying a monthly balance. This study also found that:

- 60% experienced surprise at how high their balance had reached and 40% said they've charged items knowing they did not have the money to pay the bill.

- Only 17% said they regularly paid off all cards each month, and another 1% had parents, a spouse, or other family members paying the bill. The remaining 82% carried balances and thus incurred finance charges each month.

- Two-thirds of survey respondents said they had frequently or sometimes discussed credit card use with their parents. The remaining one-third, who had never or only rarely discussed credit cards with parents, were more likely to pay for tuition with a credit card and were more likely to be surprised at their credit card balance when they received the invoice.

- Eighty-four percent of undergraduates indicated they needed more education on financial management topics.

In fact, 64% would have liked to receive information in high school and 40% as college freshmen.

Don't let your child be in the majority—explain how debt works so that he doesn't ending up feeling like the 84% who need more financial management education.

Buying A House

At this age, many young adults start looking to buy a house. As we discussed, getting a loan to purchase a house (a mortgage) is a good debt. Purchasing a house makes financial sense for a number of reasons. Over a long period of time real estate and home value appreciates. However, just like investing in the stock market, this increase is not a given every year. If you plan on living somewhere for a short period of time (less than five years), it might make more sense to rent since you will not have to worry about selling your house when it is time to move. A second advantage of owning a home is, once you pay it off, you will have a place to live rent-free for the remainder of your time in that house. In addition, if you do decide to sell and move somewhere else, you will have equity in this house, and thus, make money from this sale to be used for a future purchase. I know that this does not always happen (from the latest headlines most of us know that millions are underwater on their home loans so this is not the case for them), but if you play this correctly, many will benefit from owning a house over a period of time.

To briefly illustrate this, let's say you decide to rent rather than own a home. We will say this rent comes to $750/month. This adds up to a total of $9,000 spent on housing each year. Let's say you live here for ten years and then decide to move.

That would be a grand total of $90,000 spent on rent with nothing to show for it. On the flip side, we will say you bought this same house instead. We'll say you bought it for $100,000 and took out a 15-year loan with a 4% interest rate. Using these terms, you would have around the same monthly payment—$750—as the rent. After ten years you decide to move. We will go low and say your house slightly increases in value over this period of time and is now worth $110,000. Since you have been making monthly payments on this debt, you now owe only a little over $40,000 on this loan. After selling this house for $110,000, you will walk away with $70,000.

An argument I have heard against owning a home is you could save a lot more money if you lived in an inexpensive rental home and saved the money that would otherwise be used on a mortgage payment. While this does hold true, how many people do you know who would actually use this strategy? If you are like me, you would say not many. Most of us may have the best intentions but something comes up and we find ways to spend this "extra" money. In the long-run, most of us would spend this money on something that would be long gone after a few months, and thus, would be a costly financial mistake.

If your child feels that buying a house makes sense, the most important factor to consider is how much house he can afford. In addition to the mortgage payment, your child will also have to pay property taxes and insurance—these can be added to the monthly mortgage payment which is known as an Escrow account. Before the housing market crash, the maximum-sized mortgage many could obtain was determined by a formula related to one's income. However, the rules did change and many lenders were giving loans to people who had no business getting qualified for that large of an amount.

This is where your child needs to be careful and honest with himself. If someone makes $50,000 a year, there is no way he can afford a $500,000 house. Yes, there are exotic loans out there that could possibly allow this to happen, but after all is said and done, many people who made such decisions ended up losing their homes.

Finding affordable housing is the best thing your child can do to improve his financial situation since most of the average person's income goes towards housing. While every-day things can add up to a lot of money, buying a home that is below your means is a guaranteed way to free up more cash than cutting out those every day trips to Starbucks. (If only we could keep this in mind as we advance through life!)

Many people looked at owning a house as the American Dream and stretched themselves way too thin. What was once their dream became a nightmare after something unexpected happened and they could no longer afford their mortgage payment. In my life, living below my means has led to what I think is truly the American Dream—the ability to pursue your passions, and ultimately, happiness.

According to the Bureau of Labor Statistics' Consumer Expenditure Survey, housing accounted for one-third of American households' spending in 2010. Many Realtors suggest that one can spend one-third of his gross pay on housing. That does hold true for many who are in the low-moderate income bracket. There are many who gross around $50,000 a year and search for homes in the $150,000 range. However, this logic seems to go out as we make more money. I know of some who make $100,000 a year yet search for $400,000 homes. It seems as we make more money, we spend a greater percentage of our gross pay on our home. This limits one's options in life.

When Tracy and I married, we both felt strongly about her being able to stay home when we eventually had children. Knowing this, we settled on a house way below our means and what we would have "qualified" for. We had planned on having Tracy stay at home for one year, but after a year, we realized it best for our family to have her stay home as many years as possible. I am proud to write that she was actually able to be a full-time stay-at-home mom for nine years until our youngest daughter entered kindergarten. This was possible because we did not extend ourselves and spend as much as we could have on our houses. Some choose to live so large that they have no money left over to take vacations or even go out to eat. Pointing this out to your child before he buys a house can help him see that this decision could pay dividends for years to come.

Once your child is ready to make that purchase, he should understand that there are two major types of mortgages— adjustable interest rate and fixed interest rate. An adjustable rate mortgage (you have also probably heard of its shortened version, an ARM) has an interest rate that changes, or as the name implies, adjusts. This rate is linked to interest rate movements, and thus, has an ever-changing interest rate. What this means for the borrower is that his monthly payment will change over time.

This type of loan got many into trouble. Some purchased a home using a 5-year ARM with a low interest rate. Once this rate adjusted, some found their monthly payments increased by as much as $500/month. Many people live paycheck-to-paycheck so this sudden drastic increase led to financial trouble. On the other hand, a fixed-rate mortgage is exactly what it sounds like—a rate that stays fixed for the life of the loan. I feel this is the best choice for most homeowners since you will know exactly how much your mortgage payment will be for the life of your loan—there is no sudden increase in the payment amount. An advantage of ARMs over fixed-rate mortgages was the interest rate of these loans. Many ARMs had very low interest rates before they adjusted. However, as I am writing this, the interest rates for fixed rate mortgage loans are at record lows; many are around four percent, which to me, makes these the ideal loans to get.

In addition to the type of mortgage to choose, your child will also have to decide amongst many different mortgage features and choices. Two of the most critical are:

Points – In addition to the interest that homeowners pay each month when they write a check for their mortgage, homeowners are also charged a one-time interest payment known as points. One point is equal to 1% of the total amount of the loan. For example, we will say your child wants to buy a house that sells for $100,000 and the loan that the lender is offering charges 2 points. This will mean that your child will pay $2,000 (2% of $100,000) upfront to qualify for this loan. If your child is willing to pay more points, the lender lowers the overall interest rate. This can make sense if your son plans on staying put for a long time since his monthly payment would be lower with this decrease in the amount of interest he is paying.

Fees – When your child purchases a house, the lender will charge fees for things such as appraising the property, obtaining a credit report and processing the loan. These fees are paid upfront (like points) so your child needs to be prepared for these and budget them in when he is making this purchase.

Life is not always fair—the sooner your child gets this, the better. Some people have it easier than others, and while it may not be "fair," there is really nothing we can do to change this. The thing your child does have control over is to take advantage of the opportunities that arise. One person who made the most of an opportunity was Martha Berry.

Martha Berry is the founder of Berry College located in Mount Berry, Georgia. It is now a four-year college that spans more than 26,000 acres, making it the largest continuous college campus in the world. However, it did not start off this great.

In 1902, Berry College got its start as the Boys Industrial School. The student population and school grew rapidly. To meet community needs, expansion and money became essential. Hearing that Henry Ford was making endowments to worthy causes, Martha Berry finally got a chance to visit and talk with Ford to request money for her school; many would say that she failed at convincing him of her school's importance. You see, many people were asking Mr. Ford for money to support their cause and he was getting fed up at being a donation target. After Ms. Berry finished her pitch, Henry Ford reached into his pocket, grabbed a dime and flung it on his desk, saying, "This is all the money I have in my pocket. Take it and leave."

Many people would have been extremely upset and might have even thrown this dime onto the sidewalk upon leaving Mr. Ford's office. However, Martha Berry took this dime and used it to buy seeds for her school. One year later, she went back to Ford and showed the multimillionaire pictures of the gardens, crops and trees she planted thanks to his dime. Ford was so impressed, he gave Berry $25,000 on the spot; an unheard of fortune in that day. He later went on to build the Ford buildings, a cluster of Gothic edifices on the campus. In addition, The Ford Foundation recently gave Berry College a $9.4 million grant. All this from a dime. Sometimes life does throw us a curveball and the best we can do is put it into play and see what happens.

Embracing Failure

This might be the most important lesson you can teach your child. No matter what area of life we are looking at, it is not fun to think about failing. We never set off trying to accomplish something thinking we are not going to succeed. However, failure can sometimes be the greatest thing to happen to us in the long run if we take the time to learn from where we went wrong and move on using this knowledge to help avoid similar mistakes in the future. The following stories show five people who embraced and learned from their failures to achieve great success.

Mark Cuban

He started off his working career with little success. His parents wanted him to have a normal job so he tried carpentry and hated it. He was a short order cook, but not a good one; and even waited tables but couldn't open a bottle of wine. He eventually became a salesperson for one of the first PC software retailers but was terminated less than a year later.

Cuban then started a company, MicroSolutions, with support from his previous customers. In 1990, he sold this company for $6 million. In 1995, Cuban and fellow Indiana University alumnus Todd Wagner started Audionet which became Broadcast.com in 1998. By 1999, Broadcast.com had grown to 330 employees and was acquired by Yahoo! for $5.9 billion in Yahoo! Stock.

Cuban is now owner of the National Basketball Association's Dallas Mavericks, Landmark Theatres and Magnolia Pictures, and is also the chairman of the HDTV cable network HDNet. In addition, as of 2011, Cuban is No. 459 on *Forbes*' list of "World's Richest People" with a net worth of $2.3 billion.

Even though he failed, Cuban has this to say of these failures, "I've learned that it doesn't matter how many times you failed." Cuban continued, "You only have to be right once. I tried to sell powdered milk. I was an idiot lots of times, and I learned from them all."

Stephenie Meyer

The author of the *Twilight* series had never written even a short story before *Twilight* and had considered going to law school because she felt she had no chance of becoming a writer; she later noted that the birth of her oldest son Gabe changed her mind, saying, "Once I had Gabe, I just wanted to be his mom." Before becoming an author, Meyer's only professional work was as a receptionist in a property company.

Meyer says that the idea for *Twilight* came to her in a dream on June 2, 2003. The dream was about a human girl and a vampire who was in love with her but thirsted for her blood. Based on this dream, Meyer wrote the draft of what is now Chapter 13 of the book. In a matter of three months she had transformed her dream into a complete novel, though she claims that she never intended to publish *Twilight* and was writing for her own enjoyment. Her sister's response to the book was enthusiastic and she persuaded Meyer to send the manuscript to literary agencies.

Of the 15 letters she wrote, five went unanswered, nine brought rejections, and the last was a positive response from Jodi Reamer of Writers House. Eight publishers competed for the rights to publish *Twilight* in a 2003 auction. By November, Meyer had signed a $750,000 three-book deal with Little, Brown and Company. As they say, the rest is history. The *Twilight* novels have gained worldwide recognition and sold over 100 million copies globally. Meyer was the best-selling author of 2008 and 2009 in America, having sold over 29 million books in 2008 and 26.5 million books in 2009.

Meyer was ranked #49 on *Time* magazine's list of the "100 Most Influential People in 2008" and was included in the *Forbes* Celebrity 100 list of the world's most powerful celebrities in 2009, entering at #26. Her annual earnings exceeded $50 million. In 2010, *Forbes* ranked her as the #59 most powerful celebrity with annual earnings of $40 million. Not too bad after being rejected 14 times!

Steve Jobs

Many will remember Steve Jobs for his great success in leading Apple and the wonderful products created under his leadership. However, he should also be remembered for his failures and how these can sometimes lead to great success.

Although we have mentioned how important a college degree can be, it is not a guarantee of success. In fact, Steve Jobs never graduated from college. He only made it through about six months at Reed College before dropping out because he thought it was too expensive for his middle-class parents. Jobs was even fired from Apple (which he co-founded in his garage) after a power struggle in which the board of directors sided with John Sculley, a former Pepsi executive who had been brought in to run the company. In his Stanford commencement speech, Jobs recalled the devastating public humiliation of being ousted, and conceded that he even considered running away from Silicon Valley. Only later did he see how the blow helped him.

"I didn't see it then, but it turned out that getting fired from Apple was the best thing that could have ever happened to me. The heaviness of being successful was replaced by the lightness of being a beginner again, less sure about everything. It freed me to enter one of the most creative periods of my life. [...] Sometimes life hits you in the head with a brick. Don't lose faith. I'm convinced that the only thing that kept me going was that I loved what I did."

Instead of running away, during his time away from Apple Jobs bought the animation studio Pixar and started the computer company NeXT. Pixar revolutionized animated moviemaking with releases such as "Toy Story," "Finding Nemo" and "Cars." It later was sold to The Walt Disney Company. NeXT wasn't quite as successful as Pixar. Jobs' dream of a pricey, beautiful computer, dubbed the Cube because of its shape, never found its niche. The company's software also wasn't widely adopted.

In a 1991 article, *Forbes* said Jobs "has made fundamentally wrong decisions that could well doom the venture." Julia Pitta, author of this story, went on to say, "None of this is to deny Jobs the credit due him for what he did in cofounding Apple. But there are very few miracle workers in the business world, and it is now clear that Steve Jobs is not one of them."

Despite being labeled a failure, NeXT was an important stepping stone for Jobs. In 1997, Apple bought NeXT and incorporated some of the company's technology into its products. The deal also brought Jobs back to the company and he eventually took over as CEO. When Jobs returned to Apple, many were questioning whether Apple was beyond salvation, as the company wallowed in financial losses and seemed to have lost direction. I think it is now safe to say that Steve Jobs proved his critics wrong and used his failures to create success.

Jake Owen

Joshua "Jake" Owen was born in Vero Beach, Florida in 1981. Jake had a love of golf and wanted to become a professional golfer. After graduating from Vero Beach High School, he attended Florida State University. While there, he had a wakeboarding accident that resulted in reconstructive surgery. This surgery left Jake unable to play golf anymore. Although I am sure this devastated him, Jake did not wallow in pity. This injury might have been the best thing that ever happened to him.

While recovering from his injuries, Jake borrowed a neighbor's guitar and began to teach himself how to play it. After seeing a guitarist perform at a campus bar, he asked the bar's owner if he could play a gig there. Eventually, he became a regular at the bar, and soon took up writing his own material as well. He then moved to Nashville, Tennessee, and in 2005 signed with RCA Records.

In early 2006, Jake Owen released his debut single, entitled *Yee Haw*. This song reached number 16 on the Billboard Hot Country Songs chart and became the lead-off single on his debut album, *Startin' with Me*. The album's title track was released as his second single and became his first Top Ten hit.

Jake's second album, *Easy Does It*, was released in early 2009 and debuted at #2 on the Billboard Top Country Albums and #13 on the Billboard 200. The lead-off single to the album, *Don't Think I Can't Love You* became his first Top 5 country hit, reaching #2 on the Hot Country Songs chart in April

2009. The title track to the album *Barefoot Blue Jean Night* became his first Number One single on the country chart. A second single, *Alone with You*, reached Number One on the country chart in March 2012.

Jake has had great success that probably would not have happened if he had not gotten injured. He is someone who turned life's misfortunes into something positive. I enjoy listening to his music and have somewhat of a connection to Jake since we are both Fighting Indians; both of us graduated from Vero Beach High School.

Dawn Loggins

How does Dawn Loggins compare to the previous names? After reading her story I bet you might think she is more successful than a lot of the well-known individuals listed before her.

Dawn grew up in a run-down home with no electricity or running water. She often went days and sometimes weeks without showering. She, along with her brother Shane, would walk 20 minutes to a public park to get water. "We would get water jugs and fill them up at the park, using the spigots in the bathroom. And we would use that to flush the toilet or cook with. Stuff like that," she says.

When Dawn was a junior in high school, she started attending Burns High in Lawndale, North Carolina. This was her fourth high school because she moved quite frequently. Since Dawn was constantly on the move she had missed several months' worth of class work when she first arrived in 2010. A guidance counselor saw potential in Dawn early on and enrolled her in online classes so that she could catch up to her classmates. This work paid off.

In the summer of 2011, Dawn was invited to attend a

prestigious six-week residential summer program, the Governor's School of North Carolina, at Meredith College in Raleigh, 200 miles east of Lawndale, to study natural science. This program is reserved for the state's top students. The same counselor who first saw Dawn's potential drove her to Raleigh to attend the elite program. Unfortunately, the situation at Dawn's home would worsen while she was away. There was an eviction notice on her house during this time. At the summer program, Dawn saw her parents for 30 minutes during a short break. They talked about her school and how she was doing. Nothing seemed different. It turned out there was some trouble. She would not hear from them again for weeks.

As Dawn prepared to leave the summer program, she kept calling her parents' phone, but it had been disconnected. Her counselor picked her up and brought her back to Lawndale. By the time Dawn returned to her home, her grand-mother had been dropped off at a local homeless shelter and her brother and parents had just upped and left. She later found out they had moved to Tennessee. Dawn was aban-doned, but she was not upset at her parents. In fact, she used her parents' example to drive her and said, "I just realize that they have their own problems that they need to work through. They do love me; I know they love me. They just don't show it in a way that most people would see as normal."

For some time, Dawn lived on the couch at friends' homes while she figured out what to do. The only thing that mattered was that she would be able to stay at Burns High where she was active in extracurricular activities, had a boyfriend and a job. Her classmates there didn't make fun of her like they did when she was in middle school. "It was the worst. That's when I would come home crying because the teasing was so bad," Dawn recalled. She lived with her grandmother until she was 12 and attended junior high at a school about an hour away from Lawndale during that time. Dawn says this about that time, "My grandma loved me and she taught me a lot. She had lots of crafts around and watched History Channel with us. But she never really explained to me and my brother the importance of bathing regularly. And our house was really disgusting. We had cockroaches everywhere. And we had trash piled literally two feet high. We'd have to step over it to get anywhere in the house." Dawn would go without showering two to three months at a time and wear the same dress to school for weeks straight. "When I was little, it seemed normal to me. I didn't realize that other families weren't living the same way I was. And because of that I got teased, the kids would call me dirty."

With her parents in Tennessee, Dawn processed her options with her guidance counselor. She could move to Tennessee to be with her mother or she could be turned over to the Department of Social Services which might cause her to be uprooted and moved once again. Dawn wanted to stay at Burns so her counselor placed a call to Sheryl Kolton, a custodian and bus driver for Burns Middle School, and asked her if Dawn could come live with her and her husband, Norm. The Koltons agreed to take her in.

Now in a stable environment, Dawn was able to focus on her future—attending college. She knew she wanted a different path than her parents. "When I was younger, I was able to look at all the bad choices—at the neglect, and the drug abuse, and everything that was happening—and make a decision for myself that I was not going to end up like my parents, living from paycheck to paycheck."

Dawn applied to four colleges within the state: the University of North Carolina at Chapel Hill; North Carolina State

University; Davidson College; and Warren Wilson College. In December, she sent one final application off in the mail, to her reach-for-the-stars choice, Harvard.

No one from Burns High had ever been accepted to the elite Ivy League school. When asked why she did this, Dawn replied, "I thought about it and just figured, *Why not?*" She asked her history teacher, Larry Gardner, for a recommendation letter. "I don't know how many times I started that letter of recommendation," he recalls. "Because how do you articulate her story into two pages? How do you explain this is a young lady who deserves a chance but hasn't had the opportunities?" But after a prayer for wisdom, the words flowed. "Once again, words fail me as I attempt to write this letter of recommendation," Gardner began. "I can promise I've never written one like this before and will probably not write one like this again. Because most students who face challenges that are not even remotely as difficult as Dawn's give up. This young lady has, unlike most of us, known hunger. She's known abuse and neglect, she's known homelessness and filth. Yet she's risen above it all to become such an outstanding young lady." Months passed. She was accepted to the four schools in North Carolina. Each time, the acceptance letter came as part of a thick package with fat brochures and congratulatory notes.

After anxiously waiting for months, a letter from Harvard arrived. However Dawn's initial joy turned to disappointment because this letter arrived in a regular-sized envelope— the sure sign of rejection. Cautiously, she opened it: "Dear Ms. Loggins, I'm delighted to report that the admissions committee has asked me to inform you that you will be admitted to the Harvard College class of 2016. ... We send such an early positive indication only to outstanding applicants ..." She gasped when she read those words. Gardner had the same reaction when she handed him the note at school the next day. "I just looked up at her, and kind of teared up because this is a young lady who ..." he stopped, his voice breaking. "When I first met her and had her brother in class, they were living in a home without electricity, without running water, they were showering at a local park in a restroom after most of the people at the park had left. This is a young lady who's been through so much and for her to receive this letter—pretty awesome." Not only was Dawn accepted to Harvard, she got a full ride. She was offered tuition, room and board, as well as assistance finding an on-campus job.

After Dawn's story came out, she attracted much attention and has received notes of support along with money. Dawn wants to use this money to start a nonprofit organization to help other teens who've had obstacles in their educations. "There are so many kids whose futures aren't so sure, and they need help more than I do," she says. "I want them to be able to use my story as motivation. And I want the general public to realize that there are so many kids who need help." Dawn has learned lessons that are not taught in school. "I love my parents. I disagree with the choices that they've made. But we all have to live with the consequences of our actions. If I had not had those experiences, I wouldn't be such a strong-willed or determined person."

I think when Dawn's final chapter is written, she might have a greater impact than even she dreams of.

Quotes About Failure

It is pretty much a given that your child will face some sort of failure in his life. Here are some quotes you can share to motivate him during this rough patch:

"I have missed more than 9,000 shots in my career. I have lost almost 300 games. On 26 occasions I have been entrusted to take the game-winning shot, and I missed. I have failed over and over and over again in my life. And that is why I succeed."
—MICHAEL JORDAN

"There are no secrets to success. It is the result of preparation, hard work, and learning from failure." —COLIN POWELL

"Failures are finger posts on the road to achievement." —C.S. LEWIS

"Failure is success if we learn from it." —MALCOLM FORBES

"If you're not failing every now and again, it's a sign you're not doing anything very innovative." —WOODY ALLEN

"The better a man is, the more mistakes he will make, for the more new things he will try. I would never promote to a top-level job a man who was not making mistakes...otherwise he is sure to be mediocre." —PETER DRUKER

"One's best success comes after his greatest disappointments." —HENRY WARD BEECHER

"A man's doubts and fears are his worst enemies." —WILLIAM WRIGLEY JR.

"Remember, you only have to succeed the last time." —BRIAN TRACY

"Failure is the opportunity to begin again more intelligently." —HENRY FORD

"Failures are divided into two classes—those who thought and never did, and those who did and never thought."
—JOHN CHARLES SALAK

"Many of life's failures are men who did not realize how close they were to success when they gave up." —ANONYMOUS

"I think everyone should experience defeat at least once during their career. You learn a lot from it." —LOU HOLTZ

"Success is not permanent. The same is also true of failure."
—DELL CROSSWORD

"In order to succeed, you must first be willing to fail."
—ANONYMOUS

"The only real failure in life is the failure to try."
—ANONYMOUS

"When one door closes another door opens; but we often look so long and so regretfully upon the closed door, that we do not see the ones which open for us." —ALEXANDER GRAHAM BELL

"It is not failure itself that holds you back; it is the fear of failure that paralyzes you." —BRIAN TRACY

"Don't fear failure so much that you refuse to try new things. The saddest summary of a life contains three descriptions: could have, might have, and should have." —LOUIS E. BOONE

"I'd rather be a failure in something that I love than a success in something that I hate." —GEORGE BURNS

"I don't know the key to success but the key to failure is to try to please everyone." —BILL WILLIAM HENRY COSBY

"In order to succeed you must fail, so that you know what not to do the next time." —ANTHONY J. D'ANGELO

"The only real failure in life is one not learned from." —ANTHONY J. D'ANGELO

"Most people achieved their greatest success one step beyond what looked like their greatest failure." —BRIAN TRACY

"A man is a success if he gets up in the morning and gets to bed at night, and in between he does what he wants to do." —BOB DYLAN

"The great dividing line between success and failure can be expressed in five words: "I did not have time." —FRANKLIN FIELD

"Before success comes in any man's life he is sure to meet with much temporary defeat and, perhaps, some failures. When defeat overtakes a man, the easiest and most logical thing to do is to quit. That is exactly what the majority of men do." —NAPOLEON HILL

"The majority of men meet with failure because of their lack of persistence in creating new plans to take the place of those which fail." —NAPOLEON HILL

"An inventor fails 999 times, and if he succeeds once, he's in. He treats his failures simply as practice shots." —CHARLES FRANKLIN KETTERING

"Failure is the foundation of success, and the means by which it is achieved." —LAO TZU

"My great concern is not whether you have failed, but whether you are content with your failure." —ABRAHAM LINCOLN

"Failure is a prerequisite for great success. If you want to succeed faster, double your rate of failure." —BRIAN TRACY

"I've come to believe that all my past failure and frustration were actually laying the foundation for the understandings that have created the new level of living I now enjoy." —ANTHONY ROBBINS

"You may be disappointed if you fail, but you are doomed if you don't try." —BEVERLY SILLS

College Is Not The End of The Road

If/when your child graduates from college, he definitely deserves some praise. It is a great accomplishment but a degree does not automatically guarantee success. In fact, it is just the beginning of the path on the road to success. There is a lot more to being successful than just being smart or earning a degree or some letters after your name.

In his book *Outliers: The Story of Success*, Malcolm Gladwell argues that an IQ above 120 (this IQ is considered above average/bright) has little correlation to real-world success. This holds the same for grades. Beyond a moderate level of academic learning, there is not much evidence that grades correlate to success in the real world. I am not saying that striving for good grades is not important, but the end result is not what is most important; the important lesson is often what we learned to get that result.

Gladwell discusses a Michigan Law School study which found that minority students who, because of affirmative action, were admitted despite having lower grades and test scores, went on to have law careers as successful as their white counterparts even though they earned lower grades in law school.

Gladwell also compares the lives of two men considered to be geniuses based on their IQs. Chris Langan, referred to as "the smartest man in America," has an IQ over 200. Despite being so smart, I bet many of you have never heard of him. On the other hand, there is Robert Oppenheimer who was the scientific director of the Manhattan Project and is called the "father of the atomic bomb." Both of these men were extremely intelligent but one had a great impact on the history of the world whereas the other had little influence. What is the difference between these two? According to Gladwell, Oppenheimer practiced "things like knowing what to say to whom, knowing when to say it, and knowing how to say it for maximum success." On the other hand, Langan did not possess such knowledge, and thus, has had much less impact than Oppenheimer.

Many of us know someone who is extremely "smart" but has made little contribution to society and has not used his intelligence to the best of his abilities. We also know people who have gotten the most out of their talents despite not having the same abilities of others. This shows that while being born with smarts can help, it does not guarantee success.

Michael Ellsberg gives some great insight in his book *The Education of Millionaires: It's Not What You Think and It's*

Not Too Late. He writes the following concerning college and life after college:

"Even though you may learn many great things in college, your success and happiness in life will have little to do with what you study there or the letters after your name once you graduate. It has to do with your drive, your initiative, your persistence, your ability to make a contribution to other people's lives, your ability to come up with good ideas and pitch them to others effectively, your charisma, your ability to navigate gracefully through social and business networks and a total, unwavering belief in your eventual triumph, throughout all the ups and downs, no matter what the naysayers tell you. While you may learn many valuable things in college, you won't learn these things there—yet they are crucial for your success in business and in life. Whether you're a high school dropout or a graduate of Harvard Law School, you must learn and develop these skills, attitudes and habits if you want to excel at what you do. In your career, whenever you are faced with two paths, you will almost always be facing a choice between one path that is more predictable (in which you're more or less a cog in a predetermined script) and one that offers the chance to make a bigger impact (e.g., a leadership position) but has more risks associated with it. This is as true for a lawyer or corporate manager as it is for a start-up entrepreneur or a musician. Another way to see it: at any point in your career, you'll usually be choosing between one path that is safer and one path that has the potential to feel more meaningful to you, between one path that is more certain and one that offers more of a chance for a sense of purpose and heroism. It's hard to be a hero if there is no risk involved."

Wow, pretty powerful and insightful. This reminds me of the Robert Frost poem "The Road Not Taken." For those of you who forgot the words, I think they are very powerful and something you should share with your child. Here is that poem: http://tinyurl.com/TwoRoadsDivergedPoem

Many times in life, being different from others and taking that less traveled on road does indeed make all the difference. If your child thinks that one person alone cannot make a difference remind them that no one is too obscure to make a contribution. Like the saying goes, "If you think you are too small to make a difference try spending the night in a closed room with a mosquito." That one, small insect can make quite a difference in how well you sleep that night!

Summary

Your head might be spinning right now with all of the information in this chapter. There is a reason for this being the longest chapter—your child is now an adult and needs to be treated as such. This is the point where the skills you taught in previous years are starting to pay off, and if your son is still a little behind, now is the time you need to get serious (if you have not before). There is no turning back the clock—the decisions he makes at this point will most likely be felt his entire life.

You can be more frank with your child now and he can see more clearly how his decisions will impact what type of life he will live for many years. Some of the skills we covered in this chapter include:

✓ Finding Your Purpose
✓ Money Does Not Guarantee Happiness

✓ Place A Value On Money

✓ Post College Job Search

✓ The Married Life

✓ Emergency Fund

✓ Health Insurance

✓ Debt

✓ Buying A House

✓ Turning Lemons Into Lemonade

✓ Embracing Failure

✓ Quotes About Failure

✓ College Is Not The End of The Road

Even though this chapter deals with the young adult years, the lessons taught here (along with the other chapters) can continue to be re-addressed throughout life. These are timeless and will be relevant now and 100 years from now. Some of them are pretty basic, but if you take a look around you, it seems like many people have veered away from those practices that generations before us used to build wealth. Sometimes the latest and greatest way to build wealth is not the best; we can learn a lot from the basics that many have used for years to build their nest eggs.

Conclusion

I hope you now feel that you—the parent—have the tools to teach your child, no matter his age, how to handle money better. After reading this book, I hope you feel these are some of the most important lessons you can teach your child. To illustrate why this is so important, here are some statistics that show how our youth feel about financial matters:

- Almost 50% of those who closely monitor their finances say that they learned about personal finance from their parents or at home —2008 Financial Literacy Survey National Foundation for Credit Counseling, Inc and MSN Money

- Eighty-five percent of college graduates plan to move back home after graduating —Twentysomething Inc. 2010 survey

- About 34% of parents have taught their teen how to balance a checkbook and fewer who have explained how credit card interest and fees work —Charles Schwab's 2008 "Parents and Money"

- Ninety-three percent of American parents with teenagers report worrying that their children might make financial missteps such as overspending or living beyond their means —Charles Schwab's 2008 "Parents and Money"

- Around 69% of parents admit to feeling less prepared to give their teenager guidance about investing than they do having the "sex talk" with them —Charles Schwab's 2008 "Parents and Money"

- Fifty-four percent of college student respondents had overdrawn their bank account and 81% underestimated the amount of time it would take to pay off a credit card balance by a large margin —Center for Economic and Entrepreneurial Literacy Survey

- Students between the ages of 15-21 report they feel unprepared to face the complex world of the 21st Century —American Dream Education Campaign

- Teachers are often unfamiliar with financial materials and are "afraid that students will ask questions that they don't have the answers to, so they steer clear." —Financially Illiterate: Schools Not Teaching Person Finance Foxnews.com 6/18/02

- The majority of educators were not given a financial education course and feel unprepared to teach the subject —"Taking Ownership of the Future" Financial Literacy and Education Committee, 2006

- Students and parents agree that college students are not well prepared to deal with the financial challenges that lie ahead. Only 24% of students say they are prepared to deal with the financial challenges that await them in the real world —The Hartford Financial Services Group, Inc.

- More than 92% agree that it is important to have good money habits to be successful in life and believe it is important to know how to manage money to live within your means —Charles Schwab Foundation

- The majority of college students say they pick up most of their personal financial education from their parents but fewer than half of students said their parents make a consistent conscientious effort to teach them —The Hartford Financial Services Group

- Forty-nine percent of teens are "eager" to learn more about money management. Only 14% had taken a class on a financial literacy topic and more than one-third want to learn money skills from their parents —Capital One

- Eighty-seven percent of teens report their parents are their main source of financial education —Charles Schwab Foundation

- Teenagers that reported learning about managing savings and checking accounts were more likely to report having opened both types of accounts and they were more likely to save, create a budget and use money to make purchases —Boys and Girls Club of America and the Charles Schwab Foundation

Some pretty sobering statistics, but they illustrate even more why you need to get serious and teach your child proper money management.

Student Loan Horror Story

There is a pretty drastic story showing what a lack of financial knowledge can lead to. This story was written by Ron Lieber and appeared in the *New York Times* in May of 2010, "Placing the Blame as Students Are Buried in Debt."

Like many middle-class families, Cortney and her mother would do whatever they could to get Cortney into the best possible college, and they maintained a blind faith that the investment would be worth it.

In the end, however, the 26-year-old graduate of New York University had nearly $100,000 in student loan debt from her four years in college including all of her federal loans and her private debt from Sallie Mae and Citibank.

Cortney is making $22 an hour working for a photographer. It's the highest salary she's earned since graduating with an interdisciplinary degree in religious and women's studies. After taxes, she takes home $2,300 a month. Rent runs $750, and the full monthly payments on her student loans would be about $700 (if they weren't being deferred). She may be earning enough to barely scrape by while still making the payments for the first time since she graduated, at least until interest rates rise and the payments on her loans with variable rates go up.

Cortney badly wants a do-over on the last decade. "I don't want to spend the rest of my life slaving away to pay for an education I got for four years and would happily give back," she said. "It feels wrong to me."

Read the full story at: http://tinyurl.com/NewYork-TimesCollegeDebt The great news is—it does not have to be this way for your child. You now have the information needed to make sure they do not turn out like this student loan horror story. The choice is up to you.

Thank You

Thank you so much for taking the time to read my book. I hope you have found it both educational and entertaining and you are ready to make a permanent change to your family tree for generations to come. There is a quote by Frederick Douglass that I feel sums up my message:

> *"It is easier to build strong children*
> *than to repair broken men."*

Now get to work building!

Additional Resources

My goal in writing this book was to give you advice in helping you teach your children about money and how to handle it properly. I have used many personal examples to help you achieve this. Here are some additional resources that can help:

3 and up

Stan and Jan Berenstain
The Berenstain Bears Think Of Those In Need

Dave Ramsey
A Special Thank You: Junior Discovers Integrity
Battle of the Chores: Junior Discovers Debt

4 and up

Aesop (various books)
The Ant and the Grasshopper

Dave Ramsey
The Super Red Racer: Junior Discovers Work
Careless at the Carnival: Junior Discovers Spending
The Big Birthday Surprise: Junior Discovers Giving
My Fantastic Fieldtrip: Junior Discovers Saving

David Schwartz
If You Made A Million

Shel Silverstein
The Giving Tree

Judith Viorst
Alexander Who Used To Be Rich Last Sunday

9 and up

Brette Sembler
The Everything Kids' Money Book: Earn It, Save It, and Watch It Grow!

Books For Parents

Steve and Annette Economides
The MoneySmart Family System: Teaching Financial Independence to Children of Every Age

Janet Bodnar
Raising Money Smart Kids: What They Need To Know About Money and How To Tell Them

Nealle S. Godfrey
Money Doesn't Grow On Trees: A Parent's Guide To Raising Financially Responsible Children

Clark Howard
Clark Smart Parents, Clark Smart Kids: Teaching Kids Of Every Age the Value of Money

Robert Kiyosaki
Rich Dad Poor Dad: What The Rich Teach Their Kids About Money That the Poor and Middle Class Do Not

Dave Ramsey and Rachel Cruze
Smart Money Smart Kids: Raising the Next Generation to Win with Money

College Resources

http://CollegeBoard.org – For any students planning to attend college, register here to take the SAT and ACT, plus get college and financial information.

https://bigfuture.collegeboard.org – Scholarship Information

http://www.StaffordLoans.com – Stafford Loan Information

https://fafsa.ed.gov – Federal Student Aid Information

Acknowledgements

I must begin by thanking my Almighty God for giving me the gifts to help others handle their money better. I hope to continue using Your blessings to make this world a better place.

Tracy – Thank you so much for being the greatest wife and mother to my children. You have inspired me to be a better person and your unconditional love and encouragement mean the world to me.

Ava and Ella – It is because of you that I wrote this book. Thank you for providing so much material for this book. I love being your daddy and look forward to seeing the strong and beautiful women you become.

Mom, Dad, Meno and Art – Thank you for the great lessons you have taught me. You have all shaped me into the man I have become.

David – Thank you so much for giving me the spark to write this book. I know it did not work out the way we originally planned but am extremely grateful for your friendship and guidance.

Nancy – WOW, another book! You are much more than a publisher; I feel like you are part of our family. Thank you so much for all of your encouragement and support. I look forward to working on many more projects with you.

Finally, to my other family members, my friends and my readers – Thank you for all of your support and guidance.

Index

About the Author

Danny Kofke has been an elementary school teacher for over 14 years. He very recently stepped outside the classroom to share his financial knowledge with others as a retirement consultant. In addition to *The Don't Teach This in School* he is also the author of two personal finance books, *A Simple Book of Financial Wisdom: Teach Yourself (and Your Kids) How to Live Wealthy with Little Money,* and *How To Survive (and perhaps thrive) On A Teacher's Salary.*

Danny has discussed money management on numerous television shows including Fox & Friends, Fox News Channel's Happening Now, The CBS Early Show, CNN's Newsroom, Fox Business Network's The Willis Report, HLN's Weekend Express, The 700 Club, CNN's Your Bottom Line, Fox News Channels' America's News HQ, Fox Business Network's Follow The Money, HLN's Making It In America, ABC News Now, Fox Business Network's Varney & Company, HLN's The Clark Howard Show and MSNBC Live.

Danny has also been interviewed about personal finance on over 450 radio shows and featured in numerous publications such as USA Today, Yahoo.com, FastCompany.com, Money Magazine, Bankrate.com, PARADE, Instructor Magazine, CBS MoneyWatch.com, FoxBusiness.com, The Atlanta Journal Constitution, ABCNews.com, USA Weekend, Woman's Day, Consumer's Digest, CNN.com, Bottom Line Personal, Your Family Today and The Huffington Post.

Danny is living proof that a family can live wealthy on little money and he wants to show others they can, too!

To learn more please visit www.dannykofke.blogspot.com.

www.ingramcontent.com/pod-product-compliance
Lightning Source LLC
Chambersburg PA
CBHW051827090426
42736CB00011B/1678